P9-DFQ-267

DECORATING
COTTAGE STYLE

DECORATING
COTTAGE STYLE

Neva Scott

A LARK/CHAPELLE BOOK

A Division of Sterling Publishing Co., Inc.
New York

EDITORIAL
Chapelle, Ltd., Inc.
Julie Hale
Kathy Sheldon

DESIGN
Thom Gaines

DEDICATED TO
Lin De Witt

A Lark/Chapelle Book

Chapelle, Ltd., Inc.
P.O. Box 9255, Ogden, UT 84409
(801) 621-2777 • (801) 621-2788 Fax
e-mail: chapelle@chapelleltd.com
Web site: www.chapelleltd.com

Library of Congress Cataloging-in-Publication Data

Scott, Neva, 1949-
  Decorating cottage style / by Neva Scott. -- 1st ed.
     p. cm.
  Includes index.
  ISBN 1-60059-081-0
  1. Handicraft. 2. House furnishings. 3. Decoration and ornament, Rustic. I. Title.

  TT157.S357 2006
  747--dc22

                                                    2006025697

10 9 8 7 6 5 4 3 2 1

First Edition

Published by Lark Books, A Division of
Sterling Publishing Co., Inc.
387 Park Avenue South, New York, N.Y. 10016

© 2006, Neva Scott

Distributed in Canada by Sterling Publishing,
c/o Canadian Manda Group, 165 Dufferin Street
Toronto, Ontario, Canada M6K 3H6

Distributed in the United Kingdom by GMC Distribution Services,
Castle Place, 166 High Street, Lewes, East Sussex, England BN7 1XU

Distributed in Australia by Capricorn Link (Australia) Pty Ltd.,
P.O. Box 704, Windsor, NSW 2756 Australia

The written instructions, photographs, designs, patterns, and projects in this
volume are intended for the personal use of the reader and may be reproduced
for that purpose only. Any other use, especially commercial use, is forbidden
under law without written permission of the copyright holder.

Every effort has been made to ensure that all the information in this book is
accurate. However, due to differing conditions, tools, and individual skills, the
publisher cannot be responsible for any injuries, losses, and other damages that
may result from the use of the information in this book.

Manufactured in China

All rights reserved

ISBN 13: 978-1-60059-081-8
ISBN 10: 1-60059-081-0

For information about custom editions, special sales, premium and corporate
purchases, please contact Sterling Special Sales Department at 800-805-5489
or specialsales@sterlingpub.com.

CONTENTS

PROJECTS

EVERYDAY COTTAGE LIVING

OPPOSITE: **Everything about this room says comfortable cottage style. The vibrant plants and distressed furniture create a sense of stylish comfort.**

*W*hen we think of a cottage, what usually comes to mind is an enchanting little getaway—a cabin in the woods, beachside rental, or cozy summer place at the lake. Informal, laid-back, a bit rough around the edges, it's a place to be temporarily, a spot for casual vacations and weekend retreats, where the rules of dress, behavior, and decorating are all relaxed.

In the cottage hideaway, a carefree spirit rules: we can kick off our shoes, put up our feet and be ourselves. The furnishings—a delightful mix of the old and the new, the formal and the casual—reflect this easygoing attitude. Gently worn furniture and mismatched fabrics are mixed with heirloom items and classic antiques. Bright floral patterns are paired with pieces of dainty lace. The effect is unstudied yet sophisticated, spontaneous yet decidedly smart.

Creating this sense of relaxed charm in your own home is easy. Because cottage style combines the old-fashioned and the up-to-date, the pretty and the primitive, there's plenty of room for experimentation. Old family pictures, pottery and plants, vintage furniture with peeling paint—anything goes when you're decorating cottage style. It's a comfortable aesthetic that says small is better than grand, that tarnished silver is prettier than polished, that nicks and scratches add character to furniture.

This book can help you transform your living space into a cozy cottage-style retreat. Taking you on a tour of homes decorated in the cottage style, the pages that follow offer decorating ideas for every room, from the kitchen to the bath. You'll discover new ways to accessorize using items from the flea market, the attic, and the junk drawer. Old pieces take on new purpose in the cottage-style home, and we offer plenty of suggestions on how you can dust off your favorite treasures and display them to maximum effect.

In chapters on color, fabrics, and furniture, you'll find innovative methods for incorporating cottage style into every aspect of your decorating scheme. Sixteen simple projects—from assembling a cottage-style bench using the headboard of a bed, to sewing decorative button pillows and frilly chair skirts—are also included in the book, along with trouble-free techniques for antiquing furniture and creating your own floral arrangements.

Your home should reflect your personality, and cottage style gives you the freedom and flexibility to express your individual taste. So go ahead and decorate to please yourself and don't be afraid of change. Cottage style isn't about impressing the neighbors. If you have a playful

idea, then go for it. Combine the bold and the understated, the classic and the eclectic. Tradition with a twist—that's the essence of cottage style. When you're finished decorating, you'll have a home that reflects clear ties to the past while displaying a distinctly modern spirit, a home that's bright, breezy, welcoming, and uniquely your own.

OPPOSITE: **Don't hide your dish collections in a cupboard. Use old wooden boxes or books to vary the heights of your display.**

ABOVE RIGHT: **Cottage style and flowers go hand in hand. In this room, the floral motif is carried out in the fabric, dried flower arrangements, and the hand-painted plates and teacups.**

These old buttons gathered here once belonged to Grandma dear.

COZY COTTAGE COLORS

OPPOSITE: **Neutral colors such as brown, black, and white add harmony and subtlety to any room.**

Color is the key to transforming your home. Whatever it is you want to do—brighten up a room or cool it down, create a sense of space or a feeling of coziness—understanding how to use color and how to integrate time-honored cottage style color schemes can help you revamp your home.

If you're trying to create a serene, relaxed mood, or if you're going for a more spacious feel, use white or soft pastels. If you've chosen the bold and colorful route, decorate with warm colors, like red, orange, yellow and purple. Using dark, neutral colors like brown, black, and gray will add texture and make your rooms feel cozy. If you just want to have fun, mix things up with a colorful palette of yellows, blues, pinks, and greens.

WHITE ON WHITE

AN ALL-WHITE COLOR SCHEME tugs at the heart-strings, just as wedding dresses and christening gowns do. Everything seems richer in an all-white room. Whether it's used as a minor accent or as a major theme, white is an essential part of cottage style. When it comes to decorating, the combination of white-on-white is far from confining. The possibilities for blending shades and textures are nearly limitless. Putting a white-on-white room together can be an adventure. You can easily find the right accessories—cream-colored dishes, a bar of white soap, snowy white towels—and you don't have to worry about clashing colors.

OPPOSITE: **Texture can make white-on-white rooms more appealing. In this bedroom, the distressed furniture, the popcorn chenille bedspread, and the creamy lace create visual interest.**

COLOR COMBINATIONS

An easy way to find colors that work well together is to use that old-fashioned color wheel you learned about in grade school.

Monochromatic: A one-color scheme can go a long way if you play with shades, tints, and artful accents. White-on-white is a monochromatic color scheme seen often in cottage-style homes.

Analogous: Choose two or more colors next to each other on the color wheel and combine them on walls, furniture, and accessories. They can be warm hues (red, orange, and yellow), or cool colors (purple, blue, and green), or a mixture.

Complementary: Colors that lie opposite to each other on the color wheel create lively combinations. Red and green, blue and orange, or purple and yellow combinations will bring your room to life.

White accents bring
a bathroom to life.
Simple elements like
towels and soap can be
used to create a homey,
inviting atmosphere.

White dishes can be found
at thrift stores and yard
sales. They make a bold
statement when grouped
together as part of a white
decorating scheme.

OPPOSITE: A virtually colorless
room can still be rich and
warm. Here, the iron urns filled
with hops, hydrangeas, white
peonies, and fall leaves add natural texture. The faded floral
fabric on the chairs provides a
delicate accent to the all-white
color scheme.

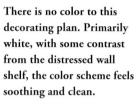

There is no color to this decorating plan. Primarily white, with some contrast from the distressed wall shelf, the color scheme feels soothing and clean.

White-on-white is a popular cottage-style color scheme, because it creates a sense of escape. As a color, white symbolizes relaxation and serenity. The ideal space to decorate in a white-on-white palette is the bathroom, a place where you can let the cares of the day fall away in the steamy calm of a hot bath.

To create that sense of escape in your own bathroom, vary the tones of white, so that the room has a rich, warm feeling. Paint the walls a soft eggshell color. Paint the bathroom cabinet a stark white to add more dimension. Then, gather up your white accessories—ceramic vases, cotton balls and swabs kept in clear glass jars, soap nestled in a white dish, white towels, and more. Once you've rounded up a nice stash of white objects and put them on display, you'll begin to see how rich and deep white can be in all its variations of tone, intensity, and character.

OPPOSITE: **A white clawfoot tub creates a striking juxtaposition when set against an exposed used-brick wall.**

SIMPLE STYLE

Nothing says simplicity like an all-white motif. Learning the fundamentals of creating a simple, white-on-white cottage-style room is easy.

Stick with one color. Paint all your existing furniture the same warm white color. The decor and the room will feel completely new covered in a calming white.

Reduce the clutter. Accessories are always a nice touch, but remember to keep them simple and sparse. Adding a plant or an accent pillow can give a room the added texture it needs.

Limit patterns. Keep patterned fabrics to a minimum, so that the eye can easily absorb the calm, simple atmosphere.

OPPOSITE: **The distressed door and wicker planter create a nice contrast in this white-on-white room.**

This bedroom is the picture of serenity and simplicity. The soft white palette is accented by the simple brown-and-white checks on the bed skirt and a subtle floral print in the quilt. The twig wreath and green fern add a dash of texture.

COTTAGE-STYLE CONTAINERS

Why stick to the traditional terra cotta pot when showing off your favorite flowers? Creative containers are easy to find. Practically anything that holds water can be transformed into a stand-out planter worthy of a beautiful bouquet. Here's a list of unusual objects that can be used to display your favorite blossoms:

Buckets and pails

Watering cans

Wire birdcages

Old shoes and boots

Stone or ceramic garden urns

Pitchers and jugs

Antique coffee pots and tea kettles

Dresser drawers

Children's toys (wagons or trucks)

When transferring your plant to a new container, make sure there's enough space in the container for adequate soil. The new planter should also have sufficient holes for water drainage. Keep color in mind when matching a plant with a container—the two should coordinate well. If you've got an especially unique container that speaks for itself, keep plant colors to a minimum.

OPPOSITE & ABOVE: **The white-on-white theme doesn't have to be limited to walls, furniture, and accessories. Creamy roses and white spring tulips add freshness to a room, especially when arranged in charming white vases or pitchers.**

ARTFUL ANTIQUING

Before you embark on this project, study a piece of antique furniture that has the look you want to replicate. Pay careful attention to the nicks and scratches that have resulted from wear and tear. You'll want to duplicate this timeworn effect.

For this project, a side table was distressed, but these same steps can be applied to any piece of furniture, or to an old door. The use of an electric sander instead of sand paper will make the distressing process easier. For extra authenticity, use tools like a chisel or utility knife on the furniture to create nicks and scratches and to scrape edges.

An easy refinishing technique, distressing is a quick way to give an old piece of furniture new life. The side table shown above was revamped in just a few simple steps.

MATERIALS:

Project to be distressed

Paintbrush

Flat warm white paint

White semigloss enamel

60-grit sandpaper

Acrylic varnish

STEP 1.

Make sure the furniture is clean and in good repair. Sand the entire piece lightly.

STEP 2.

Apply two full coats of flat warm white paint and let them dry.

STEP 3.

Apply a coat of semigloss enamel and let it dry.

STEP 4.

Gently distress the furniture with sandpaper.

STEP 5.

Clean the furniture thoroughly with a cloth.

STEP 6.

Finish with an acrylic varnish.

INSTANT ANTIQUES

Here are two more ways you can replicate the effects of time and give your furniture the dignity that comes with age. Both methods are quick, easy, and inexpensive. Get out your paintbrush and try one of the following techniques—when your work is complete, you'll have an instant antique.

Weathering: This is a simple way to make any piece of furniture look appealingly old. You'll need two different colors of paint in order to achieve a weathered look. Start with the lighter of the two colors, paint on a base coat, and let it dry. Next, add a coat of the darker color and allow it to dry. Then, use fine-grit sandpaper to rub away a bit of the darker color. This will bring out the lighter shade that's underneath. Be gentle when sanding the piece—you don't want to rub off the paint and reveal the unfinished wood.

Pickling: The name may sound funny, but this method of faux-aging furniture will give any piece a sun-bleached appearance. With a wire brush or steel wool, brush the wood in the direction of the grain, so that the grain is revealed. Then, wipe off the furniture with a clean rag. Next, using an old paintbrush, cover the wood with a coat of latex paint. With a clean rag, rub away any excess paint, leaving the paint in the grain and in the crevices of the wood. When you're through, let the paint dry, gently sand the entire surface, and clean it with a tack or lint-free rag. If you want the piece to have a more natural appearance, try covering it with furniture wax and giving it a buff.

BLUE WILLOW BLUE

THE BLUE-AND-WHITE COLOR SCHEME is a classic combination that dates back to the fifteenth century, if not before. The heritage of blue-and-white ceramics can be traced to China. Today, Blue Willow transferware from England is seen in many cottage-style homes. The great thing about blue-and-white china is that it mixes and matches well. Using several different patterns adds extra charm to any display.

Thanks to its origins, a blue-and-white palette can add a touch of formality to a room. A few comfortable chairs and lamps will make the space cozy and inviting.

A blue-and-white room is great, but a blue-and-white room with a splash of yellow or red is even better. A touch of yellow or red enriches the blue-and-white scheme and keeps it from being stark. Keep red to a minimum—it's a strong color and can easily take over a room.

OPPOSITE: **Reproducing this scene in your home is simple. Hang your teacup collection from hooks attached to the bottom of a cupboard. Place a small plant in a charming creamer. With a lamp kit and a teapot, create a unique accessory like the one shown here.**

Coordinating colors and patterns is easy to do when you've got the right pieces. In this room, the plaids and solids, the flower and bird motifs, and the porcelain pieces on the wall work together to create a sense of harmony. All of these elements are different, but they're unified by the blue-and-white color scheme.

HINTS FOR HANGING

When displaying dishes, you'll want to make sure they're securely fastened to the wall. You can attach small cloth-and-wire hangers to the back of each plate with a bit of glue. You should use a glue that adheres to porcelain. Spring-and-wire hangers can also be used. These hangers usually have clips that bend over and around the plate to keep it in place. Before hanging your plates, think of a few different arrangements for them and sketch your ideas on a piece of paper. Once you've decided on a plan, draw it lightly on the wall with a pencil. This will guide you in putting up your display.

Mixing patterns and fabrics is an important part of cottage style. There are at least seven different patterns here, yet they all enhance and complement each other.

Hand-knotted testers like the ones shown here add an old-fashioned feel to this blue-on-white bedroom. The color scheme is classic and traditional.

Cottage style is not about thinking up new ideas—it's about appreciating ideas that have worked in the past and continuing to recognize their inherent charm. Sleeping under a canopy is a cozy and romantic tradition, one that reminds us of sixteenth-century castles, Romeo and Juliet, and, of course, simple English-cottage charm.

CANOPY CONCOCTIONS

A cozy bed represents the ultimate escape—a place for daydreaming, snuggling, reading, or simply hiding out from the world. A bed canopy is an imaginative element that can provide an extra layer of privacy. Here are a few canopy ideas you can try at home:

Canopy Curtains: Hang curtain rods on the ceiling, around the edges of the bed. Then hang curtains of your choice (gathered, pleated, or tied) from the rod.

Crown Canopy: Attach a fabric panel to a shelf hung over the head of the bed. If you don't have a shelf, try stapling fabric panels to a half circle of plywood attached to the ceiling over the bed.

Covered Canopy: If you have a four-poster bed, you can drape a long, wide piece of sewn fabric over the four posts. Let it drape or tie it back.

Netted Canopy: Mosquito netting makes a great canopy. Let the fabric drape from the bedposts or hang from the ceiling.

These blue-and-white dishes are much
too pretty to be hidden away in a cupboard. They should be shown off proudly.
Here, they're accented with vibrant yellow
pears and colorful primrose to create an
eye-catching cottage-style display.

OPPOSITE: **This lovely antique
secretary makes a perfect backdrop for the blue-and-white
decorating scheme. A creamer
is filled with photos, while the
chair cushions are coordinated
with the china on display.**

WARM ACCENTS

COTTAGE STYLE, BY DEFINITION, MAY BE LIGHT, AIRY, AND ROMANTIC, but it's also about creating unexpected contrasts—especially when it comes to color. What better way to balance out those softer cottage-style color tones than with warm, sophisticated shades of brown and bronze? Dark accents can add emphasis to any room. Rich mochas and subtle tans are versatile parts of the cottage-style color palette. You can put these warm tints to work in a variety of ways.

Darker tones look especially winning when combined with white. Try warming up your walls with shades of russet or bronze, then adding contrast with white baseboards and white molding. Add accessories—candles and baskets, pillows and throws—in the same warm color scheme to draw out the contrast.

Mixing shades of brown can be fun. The different tones and layers of color add warmth and richness to a room. You can use brown on the walls or the windows, or add different shades with brown accessories.

OPPOSITE & RIGHT: **The rich brown tones create a wonderful setting. The creamy candle collection brightens the room. Brown-and-white transferware also lightens the mood.**

Brown is the perfect backdrop for distressed white furniture. The addition of wooden accents and natural baskets adds to the cottage feeling and ties the brown-and-white color scheme together.

Adding a little texture to brown paint creates a more natural background for stone accents and granite countertops.

BEFORE & AFTER

You can create cottage-style contrasts in the living room with
the right combination of colors. Choose a warm shade like dark
sand for the walls, add a snug sofa and cozy chairs in white, and
let these elements provide the foundation for the room's color
scheme. Accentuate the sand walls with accessories of the same
tone, like an antique trunk. Use warm accents like cushions or
old, framed photographs to offset the bright white of the furniture. The end result is cottage-casual.

ABOVE & OPPOSITE: **To create
cottage-style color contrasts,
start with basic pieces in white,
then add warm accents. Here,
the chairs and sofa serve as a
bright backdrop for accessories
in shades of brown and tan. The
walls are enriched with color and
offset with white baseboards.**

TRUNK RESTORATION

An antique trunk can put the finishing touch on just about any cottage-style room, adding immediate warmth and texture. If you've got one stored in the basement or attic, get it out and clean it up. Giving that old trunk new life is easier than you think.

MATERIALS:

Old trunk

Acrylic varnish

Paint (optional)

STEP 1.

Scrub off the dust and dirt.

STEP 2.

Spray the entire trunk with an acrylic varnish. Regular floor wax can be used in place of varnish—you'll need to apply a coat of the wax.

STEP 3.

Let the trunk dry.

Painting the piece is optional. Wood turnings can be attached to the bottom of the trunk to serve as legs.

It's in the Details

The importance of little details can't be overemphasized. They can make a big difference when you're tyring to create a space that's personal and intriguing.

Mix and match sizes. Cottage style acquires much of its charm from the artful display of small things. However, the use of large, oversized accessories is also important. Mix small items with chunky ones when decorating.

Experiment. Experimentation is the easiest way to find your personal look when accessorizing a room. Keep the color constant. If you're creating a black, brown, and white environment, repeat that combination over and over again.

Keep the old and the new. Nothing says cottage style more than a mix of the classic and the contemporary. Black-and-white family photos and old books look great on a new side table. The opposite is also true: modern items shine on an antique bookshelf.

Vary the theme. Don't get stuck with one kind of object—vases, dishes, candles, suitcases, or whatever it may be. Groupings of different objects create a unique and intriguing room.

Black is a great complement to brown. It can make a large room feel smaller, and a small room feel cozy. Add white to the mix to keep the color scheme from being too dark and heavy.

BELOW AND OPPOSITE: **Eclectic elements have been put together in eye-catching combinations. The large clock, antique medicine bottles, and charming rabbit figurines add depth and detail to the room.**

The official name for glass-paneled display cases like this one is *vitrine*. But whatever you call them, small, museum-style cabinets can elevate the pictures and other mementos inside to the level of prized presentation pieces. Perfect on an end table or shelf, they lend richness and warmth to a room. Shops and mail-order companies that specialize in picture frames sell them.

OPPOSITE: **Black lamps and white candles add contrast, while fresh plants give the room life.**

44   COZY COTTAGE COLORS

BALUSTER CANDLEHOLDER

One or more of these unique candleholders will literally brighten up any room. A cinch to make, they consist of little more than balusters, 2 x 6s, and decorative molding. You can paint or distress the finished product as you like.

MATERIALS:

Old baluster

2 x 6 board, for base

2-inch decorative molding, approximately 2 feet per base

Brads

Heavy-duty adhesive bond

Wood screws

Candle, 1-inch wide

Handsaw

Level

Straightedge ruler

Pencil

Drill with assorted bits, including a 1-inch bit

Miter box and backsaw

Hammer

Nail set

Screwdriver

Step 1.

Cut any uneven pieces off the baluster, then decide which end will serve as the candleholder. You want to make sure the baluster is level.

Step 2.

Drill a 1-inch hole into the center of the baluster top where the candle will fit.

Step 3.

Decide on a size for the base. Keep in mind that it must accommodate the shape and height of the baluster. If the base is wide, the candleholder will be stable. Cut out the base block from the 2 x 6 board.

Step 4.

If you're decorating the base, measure and cut the molding to fit the base.

Step 5.

Miter the corners of the molding.

Step 6.

Attach the miter to the base with brads using a nail set to tap the brads into the wood.

Step 7.

Place the baluster on the center of the base and draw a pencil outline around it onto the base. Apply a thin layer of glue to the bottom of the base and put the baluster on the center of the base. Let the baluster dry, then turn the candleholder upside down and reinforce it with a wood screw.

NUTURING NATURE

*T*raditional country charm with a contemporary touch—that's the essence of cottage style. The mood is relaxed, the look rustic yet sophisticated, and there's no better way to create the feeling than by using fresh, colorful elements from the garden and yard as accents in your home.

Part of what makes cottage style so appealing is its connection to the country, a relationship that's reflected in the use of natural colors and motifs. In the cottage-style home, you're free to blur the boundary between house and garden and indulge your passion for plants. Whether you're brightening up the den with a vibrant fern or adding a colorful arrangement of tulips to the dining room table, decorating with natural elements is a simple way to create a sense of cottage charm.

OPPOSITE: **In this room, the wooden accents and bit of greenery bring the outdoors in for a warm cottage feeling.**

A TOUCH OF GREEN

SIMPLE ADDITIONS that can enhance any home, plants are a classic part of cottage style. A little bit of green can make a big statement in a room. A pot of moss, an aromatic herb on the windowsill, a snippet of creeping fig—all make great accessories in a cottage-style setting.

When decorating with plants, don't be afraid to think big. Large plants are hearty and long-lasting. They're also a bit more dramatic than smaller specimens. Perfect for filling up an empty corner or adding emphasis to an arrangement of smaller plants, a tall ficus or rubber tree can transform a room. In the cottage style home, though, any plant is perfect if it adds a breath of fresh air.

PLANT PRUDENCE

While plants add a dose of the natural world to our homes, nothing makes a house seem more tired than a half-dead ivy or fern. Here are a few tips for keeping your plants healthy.

Don't overwater. All plants need water, but you can easily give them too much. Be sure you know the water needs of your plants. If you're not certain, call your local nursery for advice.

Prune the dead leaves. The next time you're watering your plants, take an extra moment to pinch off dead leaves. This will make your plants look greener and help keep them healthy.

Everyone needs a little sunshine. All plants do better with a little natural sunlight. Try to place your plants near windows where they can soak up some rays.

Know when to give up. If you've done everything right, yet your plant fails to flourish, it's time to throw in the trowel, as they say. Toss the plant out and start with something fresh from your local nursery.

Teacups make charming containers for miniature ivy or baby tear plants.

Easy Ideas for Adding a Touch of Green to Your Home

If you want to use plants in your decorating plan but don't quite know where to start, consider the suggestions below. The plants featured here require very little care and are ideal for growing indoors. They're low-maintenance yet attractive—perfect for adding a natural touch to the cottage-style home.

African violets: These vibrant little beauties can add a nice dash of color to a bookcase or kitchen table. You should pot your African violet in a small container filled with loose soil. Be sure to fertilize it every week. A little extra moisture in the air will help your violet flourish—try placing a small dish of water near the plant to create some humidity. African violets need about 16 hours of light each day in order to bloom and maintain healthy coloring. They also require periods of darkness—at least eight hours daily—in order to bloom. The ideal indoor temperature for African violets is about 70°F.

Ferns: The classic household plant. Ferns with hearty, substantial foliage tend to thrive indoors, while more delicate types have a harder time adapting to a sheltered environment. All ferns have sensitive fronds, so be gentle when moving yours around. Because direct sunlight can hurt a fern's leaves, put the plant in a spot where it will be exposed to low, indirect light. Water your fern regularly and mist it every now and again to add necessary moisture. The best temperature for most ferns is between 60° and 70° F in the daytime, and between 50° and 60°F at night. To keep your fern robust, fertilize it on a monthly basis, from April to September.

Philodendrons: With their heart-shaped leaves and trailing vines, philodendrons are an elegant addition to any home. Philodendrons require regular pruning, and some types have the potential to become quite large. These plants need indirect sunlight and can thrive in low light. Good daytime temperatures for philodendrons range from 75° to 85°F. Suitable nighttime temperatures vary from 65° to 70°F. You should water your philodendron regularly so that the soil remains damp. Humidity is also good for philodendrons, but they don't require high levels of moisture. Keep your plant healthy by fertilizing it on a regular basis. You can use a water-soluble houseplant fertilizer. Time-release fertilizers also do the trick.

PLANT PATIENCE

If you buy your plants from a greenhouse, where they have access to direct sunlight, be prepared for some leaf loss once you get them home. A little shedding is natural in a plant that's adjusting to a new environment and a different kind of light. If a plant is truly healthy, it will bounce back with fresh foliage once it has adapted to the new indoor setting.

Green plants add life to a monotone color scheme. In addition to providing a touch of color, they also create a natural environment that's perfect for cottage-style decorating.

A cheery touch of green brightens any room. When paired with antique or distressed items, it creates a refreshing contrast. Light-hearted and romantic, it's the epitome of cottage-style color.

Green lends a natural touch to the cottage-style home and mixes well with other hues. The distressed green cabinet shown here serves as a unique display case.

A frothy green plant enlivens an empty corner.

FLOWERING FLORALS

IS THERE ANYONE who doesn't love a bouquet of brightly colored flowers? Floral arrangements, whether they're fresh or dried, add life to a room. They're also an essential part of the cottage-style repertoire. Brightening your home with roses and carnations grown in the garden is an easy way to bring the outdoors in and create that country cottage feel.

DRYING FLOWERS

Dry the roses from your own garden or salvage them from Mother's Day and birthday bouquets. Hang them upside down in the garage for a few weeks. Don't waste the leaves—they're as important as the roses. Add hydrangea or anything else that catches your fancy. Florist's foam, sold at any craft store, is better than polystyrene foam for holding dried material in place.

OPPOSITE: **This container was made from a couple of old license plates and provides an interesting contrast to the delicate flowers. Painting the container white solidified its cottage look.**

CUP OF ROSES

A constant for the cottage look is a teacup and saucer full of air-dried roses with an old silver spoon (the more tarnished, the better).

MATERIALS:

Floral foam

Teacup and saucer

Silver spoon

Utility knife

Dried roses

STEP 1.

Cut and shape the foam. Insert it into the teacup. The secret of success here is to use the same kind of foam florists work with when creating fresh arrangements. It's soft and holds flowers well.

STEP 2.

Dry your own roses or buy a few dozen. You'll need at least a full dozen for one teacup.

STEP 3.

Insert the flowers into the foam inside the teacup and arrange them until you're satisfied with the display. Place the teacup on the saucer and add the spoon as a finishing touch.

STEP 4.

Salvage a few rose leaves and add them to your arrangement for extra charm.

A FRESH IDEA

MATERIALS:

Daisies*
Scissors
Florist's tape

Other single-headed flowers that work well include pansies, poppies, buttercups, and wild clovers.

Symbolizing the spontaneity and free-spiritedness that's at the center of cottage style, a daisy chain is an unforgettable decorative accent—the perfect addition to everything from table runners to entryways. If it's been a while since you created one of these enchantingly simple garlands, here's a refresher on twisting together a chain.

STEP 1.

Cut your flowers so that you have stems of about 6 inches to work with. If you want a tighter chain, cut the stems shorter. Just keep in mind that you'll need a little more dexterity to work with them

STEP 2.

Press the stems to flatten them, so they're more pliable.

STEP 3.

Begin by wrapping the stem of one flower behind its head, then twist the end around the stem several times.

STEP 4.

Wrap a small piece of florist's tape around the stem end to secure the twist.

STEP 5.

Thread the stem of a new flower through the loop of the first one and continue until you have a chain that's the length you need.

Vase Basics

If you're displaying your flowers in a vase of the wrong design, then you're doing them a disservice. Arranging those hard-grown hollyhocks in a container that's the right shape and size will help them look better and last longer. Consider the following types of containers when exhibiting your favorite flowers.

Tall and thin. Containers with a sleek shape, whether they're cylindrical or square, are great for holding flowers that have long, straight stems. They're also ideal for creating a clean, simple look. If you're adding just a few flowers to a tall, thin vase, then you may need to put marbles or rocks in the bottom of the container to hold the arrangement in place. When displaying a tightly packed bouquet, make sure all of the stems are trimmed to the same length. The vase will keep them supported in a tight bunch.

Low and round. A dense, dome-shaped group of flowers will appear to the greatest advantage in a low, round vase. Flowers that have branching stems and large blossoms can be paired with either a narrow or a wide-mouthed vase. Try arranging the stems in a crisscross fashion inside the container. This will create stability, and the flowers will be able to balance on the rim of the container. Low, round vases are attractive without being intrusive. If you're decorating for a dinner party, these discrete little containers can help you

conserve space on the dining room table. Your flower arrangements will get attention without getting in the way of the meal or conversation.

Flared. A flared container is just right for holding a big, abundant bouquet. Thanks to its wide, flared mouth, this kind of vase can accommodate generous, fanned displays of flowers. Flowers with sturdy stems work well in this type of container, as they add support to the arrangement. A vase that has a particularly wide flare should be filled with large blossoms to create a sense of proportion. An arrangement of small buds in this type of container can look skimpy and thin.

Bud and posy. If you don't have a full bouquet to display, don't worry. Bud vases—tall, thin, and elegant—are perfect for showcasing a single flower or a few blooms. In a bud vase, flower stems have adequate support, and blossoms stand at attention. These vases are a fundamental part of any container collection and a great way to create a simple arrangement.

DRIED TOPIARY

TOPIARY TIPS

Avoid placing your arrangement in direct sunlight—the exposure could cause it to fade. Moisture often makes dried flowers lose their shape, so keep your topiary away from damp areas, like the bathroom. To dissolve dust and dirt, spray the arrangement once a year with hairspray.

Dried topiaries provide the perfect solution for adding a touch of nature to a room. Fresh and life-like, these arrangements are light and versatile, and—best of all—practically maintenance-free.

A topiary project like this one allows you to create a custom-made accessory that reflects your taste and style. You can dry your own material or pick up a few dozen dried flowers from a florist. Add bits of hydrangea, pepper berries, or whatever you like to the arrangement to get the effect you're after. The creative possibilities are nearly boundless. Size, texture, and color—all the decisions are up to you. When you're finished, you'll have a beautiful, long-lasting natural element suitable for any cottage-style room.

PROJECT

MATERIALS:

1½ x 24-inch stick or tree branch

6-inch terra-cotta rose pot

Rocks or gravel

Plaster of paris

Spanish moss

Floral foam block

Dried flowers

STEP 1.

Center the stick in the middle of the pot. Fill the pot with a few rocks, then pour plaster of Paris over the rocks and around the stick.

STEP 2.

Neatly fill in around the top of the pot with Spanish moss.

STEP 3.

Push the floral foam block down over the top of the stick.

STEP 4.

Insert the dried flowers into the foam.

BIRDHOUSES & BIRD NESTS

COTTAGE STYLE IS ABOUT BLURRING BOUNDARIES, about making home a place of retreat, where you can relax and revive. Cottage style is also about looking for things in the natural world that bring joy and integrating them into daily life.

Almost all of us have woken up to the sound of birds chirping outside on an early spring morning. What could be more natural than reminding yourself each day about the sparrow singing outside your window? Birdhouses and bird nests are wonderful accessories that can add an element of nature to your home.

In this section, you'll find some great ways to use the birdhouse and bird nest motifs in decorating. You'll also find a few easy-to-do projects that will allow you to create your own accessories.

OPPOSITE: **Whether you buy a new birdhouse or make your own, try roughening up the painted edges with sandpaper to create a weathered look that's just right for cottage-style decorating.**

EMBELLISHING A BIRDHOUSE

MATERIALS:

Heavy-duty glue
Birdhouse
Chair leg
Picture frame molding
Drawer knob
Paint color of your choice

STEP 1.

Measure and cut the picture frame molding to the size of the house.

STEP 2.

Attach the pieces of molding to the front of the birdhouse with glue. Make sure the pieces are secure.

STEP 3.

Apply a thin layer of glue to the chair leg and attach it to the bottom of the birdhouse.

STEP 4.

Paint as desired.

STEP 5.

With glue, attach the drawer knob to the front of the birdhouse just beneath the entrance hole.

Building your own birdhouse is a unique way to add nature's charm to your home. When you're finished with this project, you'll have a one-of-a-kind accessory you can use in almost any room.

PROJECT

Birdhouses add rustic charm to this cottage-style arrangement.

Other options for making a creative pedestal include a piece of curtain rod or an old pepper mill. You can also use an old hinge or nail as a perch.

BIRD NEST & BELL JAR

A bell jar can make the most mundane item—including that sweet little bird nest you found in the backyard—look important. The pleasant decorative accent created here makes a nice gift. Because of its neutral color, it will fit in anywhere.

MATERIALS:

Bird nest

Moss

Glue

Quail eggs

Bell jar

STEP 1.

If the bird nest was found outside, you may want to bake it in the oven at 200°F for about an hour to help kill any mites or germs.

STEP 2.

Add bits of different mosses from the craft store to the nest.

STEP 3.

Glue the quail eggs into the nest.

STEP 4.

Cover the nest with a bell jar. The jar should fit snugly around the nest so that it stays put.

PROJECT

The bell jar sets this arrangement apart while protecting it from dust and harsh light.

GLASS CLOCHE

The bell jar, or glass cloche, was invented in Italy during the early 1600s. Back then, gardeners used bell jars to protect fledgling plants from frost. Today, the glass domes are an important element in home decorating. A bell jar is the ideal accessory for a cottage-style room, perfect for adding emphasis to a collection or dressing up a display. You can find them in specialty stores and thrift shops.

NATURE BOX

Decoupage is the art of decorating an object by gluing paper cutouts onto it, then covering it with a few coats of glue or decoupage medium. The coating protects the cutouts and gives the finished product a handsome, varnished appearance.

The practice of decoupage can be traced back to twelfth-century China and traditionally called for 40 layers of varnish. Today, all it takes is a few coats of glue to give an item an old-fashioned, inlaid look. You can decoupage almost anything, from a small, intimate box, to a large-scale dining room table, and just about any kind of printed material—magazines, newspapers, catalogues, letters—can provide the images and words for your project. You can also use natural elements like leaves or pressed flowers as decoration.

Before you start this project, you'll need to collect several cutouts. Stamps and postcards are used here. You'll also need to buy or make some decoupage medium. It's available at most craft stores in either a matte or a glossy finish. You can make it by mixing white glue with a bit of water.

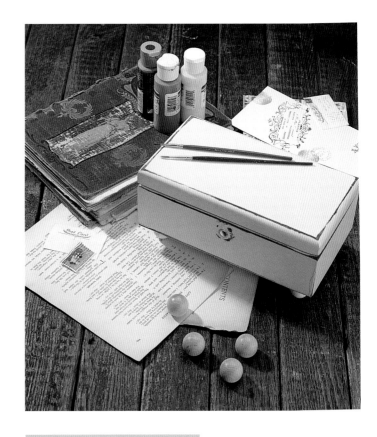

MATERIALS:

Box

Flat, warm white paint

White semigloss paint

Decoupage medium

Choice of motifs

Foam brushes

Acrylic varnish

Roller

PROJECT

Step 1.

Paint the box with a coat or two of flat warm white paint as a primer.

Step 2.

Add a coat of semigloss paint.

Step 3.

When the box is dry enough, arrange the desired motifs (stamps, postcards, dried leaves, etc.).

Step 4.

Coat the box with a liberal layer of decoupage medium. Smooth out any wrinkles or air bubbles with the roller and let the piece dry.

Step 5.

If you want to distress the box, do it now. (See Artful Antiquing, on pages 24 and 25 for instructions.)

Step 6.

Finally, spray the box with acrylic varnish.

DECORATIVE DISPLAYS

*D*ecorating in the cottage style is mainly a matter of organizing your belongings—old and new, precious and less-than-pristine—in ways that please you. It's a matter of turning plain old clutter into pleasing clutter, displaying the collections of a lifetime in combinations that express who you are.

It isn't possible for you to personally create every decorative item in your home, but it is possible to add your own signature touches to each room. Once you start, you'll find numerous ways to create cottage-style accessories for your home. Just keep things simple.

OPPOSITE: **Mismatched frames fit right in with the cottage-style decorating scheme.**

COTTAGE COLLECTIONS

ONE IS AN OBJECT, TWO MAKE A PAIR, AND
THREE COMPRISE A COLLECTION—or at
least the beginning of one. A single thim-
ble isn't very significant, but a hundred of
them is a curiosity. Why are collections so
interesting? Probably because they reveal
a lot about the people who own them.
Whether it's a bowl of old baseballs, a
ring of vintage keys, a wall of family
photos, or a tray of tarnished silver, each
collection has its own story.

OPPOSITE: **This collection of
thimbles is thirty years old.
Some were inexpensive purchases. Others are family heirlooms.**

The mirrors shown here were collected over many years.

This antique wall piece makes a nice nook for a collection of white pitchers that are both appealing and accessible.

Grouped together, these pretty pillboxes make the perfect cottage-style display.

Here, elegant perfume bottles are gathered on an antique platter.

It takes time to acquire a collection. If you're lucky, you've already inherited a group of salt shakers, dolls, or some other collectible from a family member. If not, it's never too late to start collecting. Choose an item that's fun or has personal meaning. Remember, cottage style breaks all the rules. The more unique your collection is, the better.

Items from the kitchen make up every part of this striking ensemble, including the colorful clock.

Using ordinary objects to form extraordinary displays is one of the secrets to achieving cottage style. Everyday items can prove surprisingly picturesque when arranged in the right way. The kitchen cupboard is the perfect place to find pieces to show off, and almost anything can serve as art. For an arrangement that reflects the creative spirit of the kitchen, try grouping items like colanders, bowls, and baskets. Be sure to mix colors and materials when planning your display. Combining straw and metal objects can create a lively sense of contrast.

Filling glass canning jars with staples like popcorn, cocoa, beans, or spices creates a homey feeling of abundance.

Cottage style is all about warmth and comfort, and you can easily extend this spirit to the kitchen. An atmosphere of abundance is simple to create here. Just buy some canning jars and fill them with different food staples. Varying colorful elements like white flour, yellow popcorn kernels, brown cocoa, and black beans will add contrast to your shelves.

Frames of different sizes and shapes were used to create this eye-catching little exhibit. A mix of old and new photographs adds appeal to the display.

When displaying photographs, break up larger groups to create small vignettes. These three pictures connect not only as family pieces, but because of their age, their sepia tones, their female subjects, and the silver coloring in all three frames.

If you don't have the wall space to display a collection of photos, try lining them up in a row on top of a mantel or shelf.

A collection of candlesticks makes a dramatic statement.

Skeleton keys can be found at junk and antique stores or yard sales. This collection was strung on a ring and tied to an old dressmaker's dummy.

Keys, candles, jars, frames—one is nice, but more than one is even better. Every collection adds a different kind of ambience to a room. When lit, a collection of candles creates an atmosphere of romance and coziness, while a collection of keys keeps us wondering what secrets they might unlock.

DECORATIVE JARS

There's no need to rummage around in dusty thrift shops to find unique pieces for your shelves. You can create your own collection of decorative jars using the decoupage techniques you learned on p. 68. The process is easy and inexpensive, and the end results will be one-of-a-kind.

MATERIALS:

Old paintbrush

Decoupage medium

Variety of clean bottles

Text from books, magazines, newspapers, or labels

Roller

STEP 1.

Dip the brush into the decoupage medium and spread a thin coat over the area you want to be covered.

STEP 2.

Press the text into place on the jar.

STEP 3.

Spread another thin layer of decoupage medium over the paper. Smooth out any air bubbles using the roller.

STEP 4.

Let the bottle dry, then add several more coats of the medium.

DECORATING WITH DISHES

WHO SAID DISHES HAVE TO STAY IN THE CUPBOARD? In the cottage-style home, plates and bowls aren't confined to the kitchen. Whether they're heirloom china pieces or contemporary items, dishes can be used in almost any room as one-of-a-kind decorative accents. From classic patterns, to bold, solid colors, the possibilities abound when you're decorating with dishes.

Think of a plate as a work of art. Shop for unique pieces and assemble a collection for display at home. You can show off your favorite items in a bedroom or bathroom (perhaps a small shelf of water glasses), along a staircase or on a mantel. You can hang pieces individually or in pairs. Small easels are ideal for displaying favorite plates or platters. Whether you stand the pieces up in a tidy little row, stack them under glass, or put them on the wall, they'll lend charm to your home.

These charming mismatched teacups are stacked and ready for teatime.

OPPOSITE: **Pretty dishes deserve to be seen. Display them on a tabletop or counter for everyday enjoyment.**

Rules of Repetition

Mix the old with the new. Vintage pieces take on new life when grouped with their contemporary counterparts. To create an appealing sense of repetition, use both up-to-date and antique versions of an item in your displays. The juxtaposition of old and new is a classic combination.

Create a pattern with objects. If you have objects that go together, like plates, cups, and bowls, then display them by creating a pattern of repetition. Alternate the objects along the top of a cabinet or an ornamental shelf.

Repeat colors. To create a sense of balance, repeat thematic colors throughout a room.

Same object, different sizes. If you collect a certain item, be it pitcher, plate or tea set, try using different sizes of that item when assembling your displays. Alternate large and small bowls when arranging them on the mantel.

Dishes—the very idea may seem mundane, bringing to mind cooking, cleaning, and other household chores. But in the cottage-style home, dishes play a different role. Timeless items like teacups and antique plates are a key part of the cottage-style aesthetic and can be easily integrated into your decorating scheme.

If you've got a spare set of pretty porcelain dishes that you never use in the dining room, then you've got a great resource for beautifying your home. You can put together classic displays with those platters and pitchers. To create an arrangement that's all your own, combine dishes of different colors and patterns.

OPPOSITE: **In this display, brown transferware pieces, some old and some new, achieve a charming harmony despite their differences. Transferware originated in Stoke-on-Trent, a small village in England. Today, it's popular in cottage-style homes.**

Alternating white bowls, pitchers, and plates adds an element of repetition to a room. The different sizes and shapes of the dishes add texture, as does the contrasting brown cabinet.

WATERING CAN BRACKETS

Cottage-style collections deserve extra-special display. In this project, a pair of watering cans make the perfect brackets for this cottage-style shelf. Topped with a piece of wood painted in coordinating tones, this shelf will boost your spirits whatever the season.

For this project, you can purchase pre-decorated watering cans at a home decor center or buy plain metal ones and embellish them yourself with acrylic craft paint. Just make sure that the spout of each watering can is lower than the top edge of its mouth. The shelf board will need to sit flat on the mouth of the cans.

MATERIALS:

Wooden craft board
($\frac{1}{2}$ x $5\frac{1}{2}$ x 24 inches)

Two watering cans
($7\frac{1}{2}$ inches high, 14 inches wide, and 4 inches deep)

Sandpaper

Clean cloth

Paint

Auger or awl

Wood screws

STEP 1.

Sand the edges of the board until they're smooth, then wipe off the excess dust with a clean cloth.

STEP 2.

Paint the board a color the works well with the watering cans.

STEP 3.

Determine the back sides of the watering cans. Mark two level points on the back side of each can, both about $\frac{1}{2}$ inch down from the mouth of the can and $\frac{1}{2}$ inch inside each corner.

STEP 4.

Use an auger or awl to make a hole in the back side of each can at the points you marked.

STEP 5.

Decide on a height for the shelf and plan how much space you want to leave between the two watering can brackets. Use a pencil to lightly mark these distances on the wall. Be sure the marked points are level.

STEP 6.

Fasten each watering can to the wall with wood screws threaded through the pierced holes.

STEP 7.

Set the shelf on top of the watering cans and adjust it until you're pleased with its position.

HEIRLOOM FLORAL TRAYS

The perfect complement to your favorite dishes, these floral serving trays, accented with swatches of tea-stained fabric, will add cottage-style charm to your next picnic or party. You'll use them for everything from setting out bowls of fresh berries to delivering old-fashioned sundaes to a crowd.

MATERIALS:

Unfinished wood nesting trays

Latex primer

Flat, 1-inch artist's brush

Ivory acrylic paint

Black tea

Floral fabric, 100 percent cotton

Sharp, precision-tip scissors

Matte decoupage medium

Acrylic paints in colors to match the flowers on your fabric

Small round artist's brush

Ruler

Pencil

STEP 1.

Use the flat brush to cover the trays completely with a coat of latex primer. Let them dry

STEP 2.

Cover the trays again with a coat of ivory paint.

STEP 3.

Make a pot of black tea, and soak the fabric to "age" it. When you're satisfied with the color of the fabric, remove it and let it dry.

STEP 4.

Carefully cut the flower images out of the fabric and arrange them on the insides of the trays. Let the flowers overlap onto the inner sides of the trays.

STEP 5.

With the flat brush, apply decoupage medium where each flower will be, then pat the flowers in place and let them dry.

STEP 6.

With the round brush and colored paints, add accents like stems and polka dots to the insides of the trays. An easy way to make the dots is to use the end of the handle of the brush.

STEP 7.

Use the pencil to draw curlicues or other accents on the outside edges of the trays. Paint the accents and let them dry.

STEP 8.

Cover each tray entirely with decoupage medium. The outsides will need only one coat. Give the insides at least three coats.

BOOKS, BUTTONS & BELL JARS

THERE ARE LOTS OF WAYS you can bring cottage-style charm into your home using common everyday items. If you have old books in the attic or basement, get them out and display them. They can add texture and color to your home.

Look at buttons in a new way. Glue them onto an old wooden box, or sew them onto a pillow, frame them, or just bottle them up. A bottle of red buttons can add a dash of unexpected color to a table or shelf.

Look for bell jars in specialty shops and thrift stores. Include one or more in a display to add cottage charm to a room. They're available in a number of sizes and shapes.

Opposite and Above Right:
Old books can be found at thrift stores and yard sales. Buy a few that match your color scheme and use them in your tabletop displays.

Right: **An old piece of newsprint serves as a background for a collection of buttons and keys.**

Far Right: **A bell jar can turn any item into an** *objet d'art.*

Books aren't just for reading! They can be used in a variety of ways when it comes to decorating. A neat stack of hardback volumes can add class to a room. If you've got a table lamp that isn't quite tall enough, you can add to its height by putting a couple of books beneath it. Set books on a table along with other classic elements, like a clock or a group of photographs. They'll enhance the display and accentuate the other items.

If you're in need of a few extra volumes for decorating, you can find inexpensive old books in thrift stores and antique shops, or at yard sales. Look for books with natural-colored covers for easy coordination at home.

Books bring sophistication to any display. Combine them with your favorite objects. Put stacks of special volumes under bell jars, so they won't collect dust.

Bell jars add interest
to a selection of
special volumes.

These wonderful old volumes are
stacked to the perfect height and
serve as an eclectic side table.

A button, to most of us, is purely functional—an everyday item that's most conspicuous when absent. Look closer, though, and you'll find that buttons offer a world of creativity. These cleverly designed little objects can serve a multitude of purposes in decorating. You can sew them onto quilts or pillows, or simply frame your favorites.

If you need to build up your supply of buttons, snip them off clothes that are headed for the Salvation Army or the ragbag. Sort through them and find the ones you like the most. You can combine the buttons with keys or other unique items to make a charming collage. Then, have the treasures professionally framed—you're bound to be pleasantly surprised by the finished product.

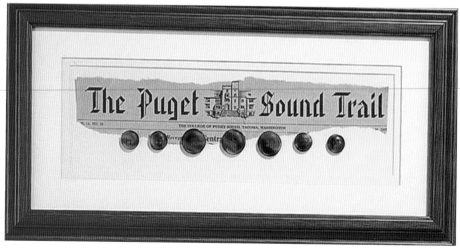

BUTTON PILLOWS

You can create cute cottage-style button pillows with just about any fabric—embroidered hand towels, doilies, dinner napkins, even an old suit jacket. Try using different fabrics for the front and back of each pillow, then adding buttons. Nothing has to match. The more whimsical your pillow, the better.

MATERIALS:

Scissors

Fabric pieces

Sewing machine and thread

Batting

Hand-sewing needle

Handkerchief or other decorative piece that can be cut in half

Buttons

EMBROIDERED BUTTON PILLOW

STEP 1.

If you don't have a vintage piece of needlework to use in this project, try embroidering and embellishing a piece of fabric yourself. This piece will serve as the front of the pillow.

STEP 2.

Cut a piece of fabric for the pillow back. With the right sides together, sew the pillow on three sides.

STEP 3.

Stuff with batting. Hand-stitch the open side closed.

HERRINGBONE JACKET PILLOW

STEP 1.

Cut two pieces of the same size from an old jacket, making certain that one of the pieces has a buttoned-pocket flap.

STEP 2.

With the right sides together, sew the pillow along three of its edges.

STEP 3.

Stuff with batting, then hand-stitch the open side closed.

ENVELOPE PILLOW

STEP 1.

Cut two large pieces of fabric to the same size.

STEP 2.

Cut a decorative handkerchief in half, either in a triangle or rectangle, depending on the shape of flap you want.

STEP 3.

Lay the pillow front right side up. Place the decorative piece right side up along the top edge of the pillow front. Place the pillow right side down over the other pieces.

STEP 4.

Sew along the top and sides.

STEP 5.

Stuff with batting. Hand-stitch the open side closed.

Glass adds class to any item: Teacups and tulips, baubles and books—everyday objects take on new importance when enclosed in sparkling bell jars. These beautiful glass domes are a great decorative tool, but they also serve the practical purpose of protecting objects from dust, dirt and harsh sunlight.

ABOVE AND OPPOSITE: **When displaying bell jars, use a variety of sizes. Here, fragile items, including the bird nest, are enclosed in small jars. A bigger jar is paired with a large arrangement of flowers.**

DECORATIVE FURNITURE

*A*s with every other element in the cottage-style home, no rules apply when it comes to choosing furniture. Old or new, painted or upholstered, whimsical or traditional, anything goes. It's up to you.

Different kinds of furniture can add cottage style to your home. For farmhouse charm, use heavy, solid-wood furniture. To create a sense of coziness and informality, choose slip-covered pieces that feature flowered fabrics. Wrought-iron or wood items embellished with shapes and curves bring an air of romance to a room, while wicker adds an earthy feel.

In this chapter, you'll find easy ideas for using paint and fabrics to liven up your furniture. These simple projects are a great way to add cottage-style charm to your home.

OPPOSITE: **When it comes to decorating furniture, fabric offers plenty of quick, creative options. A colorful print was used to make the chair skirts shown here.**

PLAYING WITH PAINT

This stool was custom-painted to coordinate with a wallpaper border.

FRUIT, FLOWERS, AND FISH are motifs frequently seen on painted furniture, but the possibilities are nearly limitless when it comes to design. Choose patterns like checks or stripes, or themes like vegetables, birds, and other animals. If you have a knack for painting, you can explore your own original ideas. Stenciling is another easy way to paint designs on furniture.

Chairs and old doors are the perfect surfaces to use in decorative painting. Doors come in a variety of sizes and make great canvases for any design. Look for old pieces with peeling paint. Use quaint cupboard doors. You can liven up the finished product with an antique decorative knob. Once you're done with your door, it will have cottage charm painted all over it.

This Della Robbia–style table is color-cued to the fabric on the seats.

OPPOSITE: **If you aren't confident enough to tackle a painting project like this floral accent table, you can achieve a similar look by simply decoupaging a piece of fabric onto a tabletop.**

All wrapped up in a big bow, this fun piece was based on the pattern in the chair cushions.

Painted tables, chairs, and stools can give your dining or kitchen area character and charm. Favorite motifs for kitchens include fruit and vegetables. You can enhance the theme by upholstering your chairs with a complementary fabric. Add a small skirt around the seat of each chair for frills and fun. The combined effect of painted furniture with upholstered seating is delightful and easy to achieve.

Painted furniture should reflect a home-owner's personality. A dining chair is an excellent medium for self-expression. On this page, chairs painted by several different artists express a dynamic, unique sensibility.

Try not to tuck decoratively painted chairs under a table where they can't be seen. If you'd like the art on your chairs to be appreciated, use a glass-topped table. A pedestal for a glass-topped table is not difficult to make—just be sure the base is heavy. A local glass shop can cut any size or shape of glass top you'd like, with either a beveled or penciled edge.

A fun way to get a unique assortment of chairs is to ask a different designer to paint each one. Give them a theme and color scheme and see what they come up with.

A glass-topped table is a great way to show off custom-painted chairs.

PAINTING PRELIMINARIES
TIPS FOR PREPARING FURNITURE

Before you start, you want to make sure the surface of the furniture you're painting is in good shape. If you're working with a piece of unfinished furniture, fill in any holes and nicks with wood filler. Use a fine-grit sandpaper to remove excess filler and completely clean the piece. Wipe off the furniture with a clean cloth and apply your first coat of paint. Sand the piece again and wipe it down. Then, apply your top coat of paint. Finish by applying several coats of varnish.

If you're working with a piece of painted furniture that's in good condition, sand the piece with medium-grit sandpaper and apply your paint. If the item has some chips and nicks, you should smooth out those areas with sandpaper prior to painting. If the piece is well-worn, fill in cracks and gaps with wood filler and let it dry. Sand the piece until smooth, coat it with primer, and apply your paint. Before applying a second coat, you should sand the piece again lightly.

You don't have to possess the talent of Picasso to make your personal mark with paint. Using one of the simple techniques below, you can easily express your individual style when it comes to accenting furniture. Whether you're painting fancy flourishes on your favorite chair or stenciling a simple pattern onto a table, you can add colorful highlights to furniture in minutes.

SPONGING

It's as easy as it sounds: just dip a sponge in paint and pat it on the surface you want to cover. The results depend upon the amount of pressure you use when painting. A gentle touch will create a light look. Use a heavier hand, and you'll produce patches of intense color. The paint you apply can provide the final finish on a piece of furniture, or it can function as the background for further applications. The use of a sponge makes it easy to blend colors and create unique effects. Try cutting sponges into different shapes—dots, stars, or circles—to produce your own patterns. You can use kitchen or cosmetic sponges, sea sponges, or sponge mitts when applying paint. For extra texture, try painting with crumpled newspaper or rough fabric.

STENCILING

A classic way to add an extra dash of color to a chair or table, stenciling is the transferring of a cutout pattern onto a surface using a precut form with holes and either acrylic or stencil paint. Precut stencils in a variety of designs are available in most craft stores, or you can make your own from cardboard, metal, or paper. To do the actual painting, you'll need a paintbrush, a stencil brush, or a sponge. Use painter's tape or a spray adhesive to hold the stencil in place, then dab on the paint, carefully filling in the cutout areas in the pattern. Stay inside the lines when painting and try not to smudge your work when removing the stencil.

STAMPING

For instant embellishment, stamping is the solution. Most craft stores carry rubber stamps in a variety of sizes and designs. All you have to do is dip the stamp in acrylic paint and apply it to the piece you're decorating.

Take cottage style outside with a set of colorful chairs. These sponge-painted rockers are perfect for the porch or yard.

Whimsy and precision are combined in this table, which has a distinctive look. The black background and bold colors make a fun yet dramatic statement.

GLASS-PANED DOOR TABLE

A glass-paned table is a great way to show off a set of decoratively painted chairs. You can make your own see-through table from a solid wood door, a French door, or a half-paned door. Legs for the table can be found in junk shops and antique stores. They can also be ordered online from furniture or woodworking suppliers. You'll need legs that are 30 inches tall. If you want your table to have an antique look, distress the door and the legs first.

MATERIALS:

Door

4 table legs, each 30 inches tall

Paint

Sandpaper

Glass top

STEP 1.

Once you've rounded up the door and table legs, have a local carpenter create a skirt and make the necessary joinery for the table.

STEP 2.

Paint and distress the table and legs to your liking.

STEP 3.

Take the table to a glass shop and have it fitted with a pencil-edged ⅜-inch glass top.

DECOUPAGED CLOSET DOORS

To add extra interest to otherwise plain white closet doors, try decoupaging a floral motif onto a couple of the panels. The motif used here was cut from wallpaper border, but you can use any image you like as decoration. Just be sure you have matching designs for each door.

MATERIALS:

One roll of wallpaper border

Decoupage medium

**Small sharp scissors
(Manicure scissors work well)**

Small paintbrush

STEP 1.

Decide which portion of the border's design you want to use. Choose a section that will look good by itself when you cut it out.

STEP 2.

Carefully cut out the design using a pair of small, sharp scissors. Cut as many additional matching designs as you need for the doors.

STEP 3.

Brush a thin layer of decoupage medium over the area where you plan to attach the design

STEP 4.

Brush a thin layer of decoupage medium over the back of the design you cut out.

STEP 5.

Position the design over the area and smooth it out with your hands. Use a soft cloth to eliminate bubbles or wrinkles.

STEP 6.

Brush another layer of the medium over the design, working from the center out toward the edges.

*Repeat Steps 3 through 6 for each of the remaining designs,
making sure to place them in positions relative to the first one.*

FABRIC & FURNITURE

JUST ABOUT ANY PIECE OF FURNITURE can be revived or reinvented with new fabric. Fabric allows you to use your imagination and opens the door to creative color and pattern combinations.

There's no particular secret to choosing fabric. Go to a fabric store and select swatches that appeal to you. Don't force your design. If it almost works, it doesn't work. Find fabric that suits your needs and taste. Sometimes floral prints of the same scale work together, and sometimes they don't. There are no rules to choosing fabric—just trust your instincts.

OPPOSITE AND RIGHT: **Floral prints are easy to integrate into the cottage-style home. With their bold color palettes and strong patterns, they can be used to tie the elements of a room together.**

CARING FOR YOUR COTTAGE-STYLE FABRICS

Linen and lace pieces require extra-special treatment. Whether they're beloved heirlooms or flea market finds, you want your prized pieces to look their best. Fortunately, those vintage textiles you treasure so much can be easily cleaned by hand at home. A few simple steps can prolong the life of your favorite fabrics and keep them looking fresh.

Lace: When cleaning those dainty doilies, avoid using soaps that have perfumes, phosphates, or colorants. You can bypass other harmful chemicals and minerals by using distilled water during the cleaning process. Lace pieces should be soaked individually in soapy water for 15 minutes. A natural sponge can be used to remove stains, but try not to scrub the fabric. After washing, fragile items should be laid out on a flat, clean surface, reshaped, and allowed to dry naturally. Line-drying can damage delicate lace.

Table linen: Wash vintage tablecloths and napkins by hand with a mild soap and cold, distilled water. Sturdy linens that are in good shape can be machine-washed on a gentle cycle. The best time to iron your linens is right after they've been washed, while they're still damp. Put your iron on its hottest setting, and press the linens until they're dry. You should never iron creases into the cloth, because the pressure could damage the fabric.

Storage: When it's time to tuck those precious pieces away, don't fold them up. Folding puts stress on fabric and can lead to permanent creasing. Instead, linen and lace pieces should be rolled up and wrapped in acid-free paper. Acid-free boxes, which are sold in most photography shops and craft stores, are the best option for storage. Plastic bags should never be used when packing items, because they capture moisture, which can lead to mildew. Cedar chests and other wooden containers should also be avoided, since they contain oils that can hurt valuable fabrics.

Be sure to rotate displayed items every six months to minimize damage from light and keep colors from fading.

Here's a handy household secret: If a spill occurs while your precious linens are gracing the table, sprinkle table salt over the stain. Those little white grains will absorb the mess.

HEADBOARD BENCH

With a little work, this old four-poster bedframe was turned into a lovely, antique-looking bench. Cushions and a batch of pillows made from a variety of fabrics give the piece extra charm. If you don't have a bed to use for this project, look for one in an antique shop or thrift store. You'll need both the headboard and footboard.

PROJECT

MATERIALS:

Four-poster bedframe

2 x 4s or 1 x 4s for bench seat

Small steel hardware plates

Screws

Paintbrush

Warm white paints in flat
and semigloss

Electric sander and 60-grit
sandpaper

Acrylic varnish

Fabric and stuffing for
cushions and pillows

STEP 1.

Have a carpenter turn the bedframe into a bench by using
the headboard for the back and
the footboard for the sides. The
footboard should be cut in half
to make the sides. A new board
will be used to connect the two
sides at the front of the bench.

STEP 2.

Sand the bench lightly.

STEP 3.

Paint the bench in warm white,
starting with two full coats of
flat paint. Add a coat or two
of semigloss.

STEP 4.

Gently distress the edges. You
can use an electric sander or
60-grit sandpaper.

STEP 5.

Spray with acrylic varnish.

STEP 6.

Add cushions and pillows to fit.

CHAIR SKIRTS

This simple project can add spunk to your dining room chairs. No matter what kind of fabric you choose—elegant, playful or casual—you can create pieces that will add cottage style to any room.

MATERIALS:

Tape measure

Fabric

Sewing machine and thread

Upholstery tacks

STEP 1.

Measure around the chair seat and cut a 6-inch strip of fabric two to three times the measurement of the chair seat.

STEP 2.

Hem and gather the fabric.

STEP 3.

Attach the fabric to the underside of the seat bottom with upholstery tacks.

Pillows in a variety of sizes and fabrics add cottage-style comfort to this cozy bedroom.

On the couch, cushions in different prints and patterns are mixed to create a one-of-a-kind combination.

If you want your home to have that cozy cottage feeling, but you don't have the money to pay an upholsterer, pillows and seat cushions are an easy answer. Pillows soften a room and make it more welcoming. They're great for tying mismatched pieces of furniture together. Pillows are easy to make in any style or size—just choose your favorite fabrics. If you already have an odd assortment of pillows, make slipcovers for them instead of starting from scratch. Then sink back and soak in your cottage ambience.

OPPOSITE: **This picture-perfect cottage-style room has all the right elements, including delicate ceramic pieces, plush cushions, and pretty plants.**

ABOUT THE AUTHOR

Neva Scott is the owner of Nest Feathers, a shop in Richland, Washington. Born and raised in Panaca, Nevada, she credits her appreciation for the humble, homey charm that defines cottage style to her small-town upbringing.

Growing up, Neva was surrounded by grandparents and loved ones who valued cooking, quilting, and other home crafts. She now sees that influence coming through in her business. Neva was featured as an Entrepreneur of the Year nominee in *Victoria's* March 2000 issue and was also showcased in *Victoria's* "A Shop of One's Own."

ABOUT NEST FEATHERS

Nest Feathers is a warehouse located in an unlikely, quasi-industrial part of town. This is the shop's third location, and customers seem to follow wherever it goes. Although Nest Feathers sells gifts and greeting cards, candles and pot-pourri, it's best known for its painted furniture. The pieces are painted white or black, then decorated by a core of very talented artists.

The inventory in Nest Feathers is a combination of the new and the old. Says Neva, "I love to mix vintage pieces from the 20s, 30s, and 40s with antiques that we have rescued from the back of some dusty warehouse. Sometimes, if we find a rich and lovely patina on a piece, it may go directly into the store. But we're just as likely to paint it white, black, green, or decoratively. Some of our suppliers shudder to think of what we'll do to a piece and frequently

say, 'Don't even tell me you're painting this 1850s Welsh sideboard!' But that is what cottage style is all about—being more concerned with effect and charm than adhering to any particular set of rules."

From the beginning, Nest Feathers has been a family affair. Neva's daughters, Erica and Jessica, worked after school, and her husband, Walter, was indispensable on weekends. As the business grew, Neva persuaded her other daughter, Monica, who'd just graduated from college, to come and manage the store.

They dedicate this book to their customers.

ACKNOWLEDGMENTS

THANKS TO THE FAMILIES that allowed us to feature their homes in this book:

> Gary and Joyce Baker
> Aaron and Monica De Witt
> Roger and Lin De Witt
> John and Debra Fox
> Reed and Ciel Murri
> Dave and Kathy Renzelman
> Walter and Neva Scott

SPECIAL THANKS to Cheri Alexander, Carl Barr, Grandpa Gray, Michelle Erdman, Susan Ballo, Roth Stromswold, Barbara Ward, Mary Hanlon, Marjorie Scott, Glen Greiner of Wild Goose Designs, Eloise Wright, Ciel Murri, Brenda Ripplinger, Jan Yancey, Terri Akins, Michelle Allgaier, Paris Rogers, and Sydelle De Witt for sharing their creative talents. Thanks to the members of my wonderful family, who have helped from the beginning, my daughters Monica, Erica, and Jessica, and my husband, Walter, who is indispensable.

METRIC CONVERSION CHART

INCHES TO MILLIMETERS AND CENTIMETERS							YARDS TO METERS										
INCHES	MM	CM	INCHES	CM	INCHES	CM	YARDS	METERS	YARDS	METERS	YARDS	METERS	YARDS	METERS	YARDS	METERS
¼	6	0.6	10	25.4	31	78.7	⅛	0.11	2⅛	1.94	4⅛	3.77	6⅛	5.60	8⅛	7.43
½	13	1.3	12	30.5	33	83.8	¼	0.23	2¼	2.06	4¼	3.89	6¼	5.72	8¼	7.54
⅝	16	1.6	13	33.0	34	86.4	⅜	0.34	2⅜	2.17	4⅜	4.00	6⅜	5.83	8⅜	7.66
¾	19	1.9	14	35.6	35	88.9	½	0.46	2½	2.29	4½	4.11	6½	5.94	8½	7.77
⅞	22	2.2	15	38.1	36	91.4	⅝	0.57	2⅝	2.40	4⅝	4.23	6⅝	6.06	8⅝	7.89
1	25	2.5	16	40.6	37	94.0	¾	0.69	2¾	2.51	4¾	4.34	6¾	6.17	8¾	8.00
1¼	32	3.2	17	43.2	38	96.5	⅞	0.80	2⅞	2.63	4⅞	4.46	6⅞	6.29	8⅞	8.12
1½	38	3.8	18	45.7	39	99.1	1	0.91	3	2.74	5	4.57	7	6.40	9	8.23
1¾	44	4.4	19	48.3	40	101.6	1⅛	1.03	3⅛	2.86	5⅛	4.69	7⅛	6.52	9⅛	8.34
2	51	5.1	20	50.8	41	104.1	1¼	1.14	3¼	2.97	5¼	4.80	7¼	6.63	9¼	8.46
2½	64	6.4	21	53.3	42	106.7	1⅜	1.26	3⅜	3.09	5⅜	4.91	7⅜	6.74	9⅜	8.57
3	76	7.6	22	55.9	43	109.2	1½	1.37	3½	3.20	5½	5.03	7½	6.86	9½	8.69
3½	89	8.9	23	58.4	44	111.8	1⅝	1.49	3⅝	3.31	5⅝	5.14	7⅝	6.97	9⅝	8.80
4	102	10.2	24	61.0	45	114.3	1¾	1.60	3¾	3.43	5¾	5.26	7¾	7.09	9¾	8.92
4½	114	11.4	25	63.5	46	116.8	1⅞	1.71	3⅞	3.54	5⅞	5.37	7⅞	7.20	9⅞	9.03
5	127	12.7	26	66.0	47	119.4	2	1.83	4	3.66	6	5.49	8	7.32	10	9.14
6	152	15.2	27	68.6	48	121.9										
7	178	17.8	28	71.1	49	124.5										
8	203	20.3	29	73.7	50	127.0										

INDEX

W9-CCT-259

ALAIN

THE ART OF COOKING WITH VEGETABLES

PASSARD

F

FRANCES LINCOLN LIMITED
PUBLISHERS

To Augustin

PREFACE

Colour has always brought my creativity to life. As a child, I could spend hours colouring, or making little collages from pieces of paper cut into different shapes. My very first work, a Harlequin, remains forever engraved in my mind's eye. And this passion for collage and painting has never left me, so that now there is a perpetual to-ing and fro-ing between a recipe and its illustration.

The collages in this book express marvellously well the influence of colour in my cooking: for me, it is a true source of inspiration, one which urges me to search for partnerships between ingredients in a quest for gastronomic and visual harmony. Most often, it is the recipe which inspires the collage – usually because it has formed an attractive composition on the plate and I have wanted to capture it on paper. But I have also enjoyed doing the reverse: thinking first about the collage and then creating the dish which corresponds to it. I sometimes have the feeling of giving a flavour to a colour, in fact.

As with the collages, the recipes have been created for this book as a special gift to my restaurant L'Arpège, which recently celebrated its 25th anniversary. A homage to vegetables, which are inextricably linked to my career as a restaurateur, the book has 48 recipes to enjoy season by season. In these pages are innovative, sometimes unimaginable, partnerships of ingredients to delight and surprise you. Many of the recipes are for starters or side dishes, but you can create a meal by combining a number of dishes from the same season, and there are suggestions for making some of these dishes more substantial.

So now it is up to you; it's your turn to be a cook and an artist with a special eye for colour. I hope you derive as much pleasure from the art of cooking with vegetables as I do myself.

CONTENTS

CARROTS AND BASIL
IN PURPLE SPLENDOUR

SERVES 4, 30MINS

2 bunches of purple carrots, such as Purple Haze, weighing about 800 g (1 lb 12 oz) topped, tailed and scrubbed

leaves from a bunch of purple basil (or green basil if purple is unavailable)

a pinch of powdered cinnamon

about 80 g (3 oz) lightly salted butter

about 2 tbls soy sauce, regular or light according to taste

fleur de sel or salt of your choice

DRINK WITH

Syrah (Shiraz) preferably a Saint-Joseph or a Cote-Rôtie

Oh, the allure of purple pigment! I love it when colour is the inspiration for culinary creation. Have fun whenever – and wherever – you select your produce. Try choosing vegetables, herbs and fruit from the same part of the colour spectrum, subtle though this might be. For me, it's a good reason to bring ingredients together – as demonstrated here. Purple basil isn't always easy to buy, but the purple Opale variety is certainly easy to grow. From early to late spring, you can experiment with groups of whites, yellows, reds or greens . . .

———————————

Cut the carrots in half lengthways, then cut across into semi-circles about ½ cm (¼ inch) thick. Over low heat, melt the butter in a saucepan; add the carrots and enough cold water to barely cover them. Put a round of greaseproof (waxed) paper on top. Stew the carrots very gently, lifting away the paper occasionally and swirling the pan to turn the carrots and coat them evenly in the buttery juices.

When the water has completely evaporated, leaving the carrots glazed with butter, sprinkle over soy sauce to taste and add the cinnamon and the basil leaves. Swirl the pan to mix. Adjust the seasoning to taste, adding salt if necessary, then transfer to a warm serving dish. This works equally well as a first course or as an accompaniment for roasted or grilled cuts of beef.

BELL-SHAPED CARROTS *with* RED SORREL AND WHITE WINE

SERVES 4, 50MINS

24 carrots with stalks

1 x 75 cl bottle of Côtes du Jura Savagnin white wine,
or other firm dry white wine

a good handful of red sorrel leaves, or green ones
if red are unavailable

about ½ tbls finely chopped fresh ginger

4 cloves of new garlic, peeled and crushed

150 g (5 oz) lightly salted butter

1½ tbls walnut oil

fleur de sel or salt of your choice

freshly ground white pepper

DRINK WITH

Chardonnay or a Chardonnay-Savagnin blend from the Jura

The sweetness of the carrot set against the tartness of sorrel makes for a good duel. In the role of umpire, I use savagnin wine – a firm, pungent white wine from the Jura which holds its flavour when cooked alongside garlic and ginger. By giving the carrots a pretty bell-shape and preserving their stalks, you have an original and elegant first course, as well as an ideal accompaniment for turbot or guinea fowl . . .

————————————

Scrub the carrots leaving their skins intact and preserving about 4 cm (1½ inches) of their stalks. Trim the carrots into the shape of little bells as illustrated in the collage (right). Keep the left-over pieces of carrot for crudités, stock or a *mirepoix*. Simmer or steam the carrots to an *al dente* stage – about 10 minutes. Plunge them into cold water to arrest their cooking, then drain again and set aside.

While the carrots are cooking, pour the white wine into a sauté pan with flared sides, adding the ginger and garlic. Boil the wine vigorously until it reduces by half. To make the sauce, stir in the butter and walnut oil and whisk it gently – preferably using an immersion stick-whisk. Season with salt and freshly ground white pepper.

Add the carrots to the sauce and simmer them very gently for 10 minutes, taking care not to let the sauce rise to a boil. Lay the sorrel leaves on top and continue to simmer the ingredients until the leaves have wilted – up to 20 minutes. Transfer to warm soup plates and serve without delay.

HERB-FILLED PEPPERS ON WARM CRUSTY BREAD

**SERVES 4, 55 MINS
PLUS 30 MINS RESTING**

2 large sweet (bell) peppers,
the colour of your choice;
cut in half, seeds and
membrane removed

about 140 g (5 oz) broad beans
(fava beans) in their pods,
80 g (3 oz) shelled

40 g (1½ oz) lightly salted
butter

2 cloves of new garlic, peeled
and very finely chopped

60 g (2½ oz) onion,
very finely chopped

2 handfuls of green sorrel,
finely chopped

leaves from ½ bunch
fresh coriander (cilantro),
finely chopped

leaves from ½ bunch chervil,
finely chopped

leaves from ½ bunch basil,
finely chopped

½ small bunch chives,
finely snipped

2 tbls virgin olive oil

1 *ficelle* or flute baguette

shavings of fresh Parmesan

fleur de sel or salt of
your choice

DRINK WITH
A full-bodied Spanish red wine

SERVE WITH
A *mesclun* salad dressed with
the juice of ½ lime

TO SERVE AS A MAIN COURSE
Simply double the portion size.

In the warmth of the oven, the *pot pourri* of herbs unleashes a barrage of flavour and scent on the sweet peppers. Perhaps because of their stately bearing, I like to serve them poised on a little base of bread - a *ficelle*, or a flute, is best for this - and leave them in the warm oven before serving, to absorb scents and flavours.

———————

To skin the broad beans, plunge them into lightly salted boiling water for 3 minutes, then refresh in cold water, and drain. Remove and discard the skins. Chop the beans finely and set aside.

To assemble the filling, melt the butter in a sauté pan over low heat. When the butter starts to foam, add the garlic and onion and, after a few minutes, the broad beans. When these ingredients have softened slightly, add the sorrel, the coriander, chervil, basil and chives, and stir to distribute the ingredients evenly. Season to taste with salt, then set aside to cool on a plate.

To make the peppers easy to peel, blister their skins evenly beneath a hot grill, turning them with a skewer. Wrap them briefly in a cold damp kitchen towel, then peel them.

Spoon the filling into the peppers and transfer them to a shallow roasting pan smeared with the olive oil. Bake in a preheated 200°C (400°F, Gas Mark 6) oven. When – after about 20 minutes – the filling is cooked, remove the peppers from the oven and turn it off.

Cut the bread in half lengthways, then across, to make 4 rectangles about 13cm (5inches) long. Put the peppers on top and return them, in the roasting pan, to the warm oven for 30 minutes, leaving the door of the oven wide open.

Just before serving, adjust the seasoning and scatter with shavings of Parmesan. Offer the peppers with a *mesclun* salad.

NEW POTATOES *with* ROCKET AND RASPBERRY VINEGAR

SERVES 4, 50 MINS PLUS 20 MINS COOLING

12 new potatoes the size of an egg,
in their skins, washed

150 g (5 oz) unsalted butter

12 pinches of cumin

soy sauce to taste

FOR THE ACCOMPANYING SALAD

several handfuls of rocket

a bunch of spring onions (scallions), very finely sliced

leaves from a bunch of chervil, snipped with scissors

a few drops of raspberry vinegar

a dash of virgin olive oil

fleur de sel or salt of your choice

DRINK WITH

A Pinot Noir from Alsace

I love this trio. But then I like to play with touches of sweetness, bitterness and acidity. This recipe unites all three elements by bringing together new potatoes, rocket and raspberry vinegar. The result is excellent and, above all, the scent is ravishing. I also employ cumin and soy sauce – flavours which find their way inside the potatoes themselves. Make sure you buy the best quality soy sauce regardless of whether it is a regular, light or salt-reduced version; it will do most of the work here in stimulating the taste buds.

———————————

Arrange the potatoes, in their skin, on a baking tray and bake them in a preheated 190°C (375°F, Gas Mark 5) oven for about 35 minutes or until tender when prodded with a skewer. Turn off the oven and leave the potatoes to cool, with the oven door ajar, for 20 minutes.

Meanwhile, prepare the accompanying salad: put the rocket and spring onions into a salad bowl. Add the snipped chervil leaves, a good dash of olive oil, a splash of raspberry vinegar and a sprinkling of salt. Toss the salad to mix the ingredients.

Remove the potatoes from the oven. With a small sharp knife, cut a small cross on top of each potato. Insert into each opening a tiny piece of butter, a small pinch of cumin, and one or two drops of soy sauce. Arrange the potatoes on 4 serving plates along with the salad. Mix the elements well to exploit the contrasts of flavour, texture and temperature.

AUBERGINE (EGGPLANT)
with GREEN CURRY

SERVES 4, 50 MINS

2 large aubergines (eggplants), each weighing
about 200 g (7 oz)

about 16 tbls virgin olive oil

1 large sweet white onion, such as a Cévennes
or a Spanish onion

leaves from ½ bunch flat-leafed parsley, finely chopped

leaves from ½ bunch fresh coriander (cilantro), finely chopped

½ stick lemongrass, trimmed of dry outer layers,
the stalk finely chopped

1 clove of new garlic, peeled and finely chopped

a small amount of finely chopped green chilli to taste

⅓ lime, skin intact

a pinch or two of Madras curry powder, according
to taste

fleur de sel or the salt of your taste

DRINK WITH

Red from the Languedoc region, such as a Corbières
or a Faugères

TO SERVE AS A MAIN COURSE

Double the portion size and offer an accompaniment
of wild rice.

This is one of the loveliest specialities at L'Arpège. It must be something to do with the tender, savoury flesh of the roasted aubergine and the multiple flavours of the mysterious green curry.

———————————

Cut the aubergines in half lengthways, score their flesh with a small knife, then drizzle over half the quantity of olive oil. Put the aubergines on a baking sheet and bake them in a preheated 200°C (400°F, Gas Mark 6) oven for 30–40 minutes, turning half way through cooking.

Meanwhile, make the green curry: in a sauté pan, sweat the onion in the remaining olive oil over very gentle heat. When, after about 10 minutes, it starts to soften and become translucent, stir in the parsley, coriander, lemongrass, garlic, chilli, lime and Madras curry to taste. Continue to sweat the ingredients for a further 10 minutes or until the onion is completely soft.

Drain the mixture through a sieve, holding on to the liquid. Discard the segment of lime. Blend the solids briefly, adding just enough of the liquid – or some olive oil if you prefer – to make a light, homogeneous purée which holds its form. Adjust the seasoning, then use a pair of spoons to shape this purée into 4 egg-shaped *quenelles*.

Present the baked aubergines, seasoned with salt, on a warm serving dish. Arrange the *quenelles* alongside. Serve as a first course or as an accompaniment to roast chicken or spit-roasted lamb. The curry mixture keeps extremely well in a sealed container in the refrigerator and makes a good flavouring for cauliflower, eggs and fish.

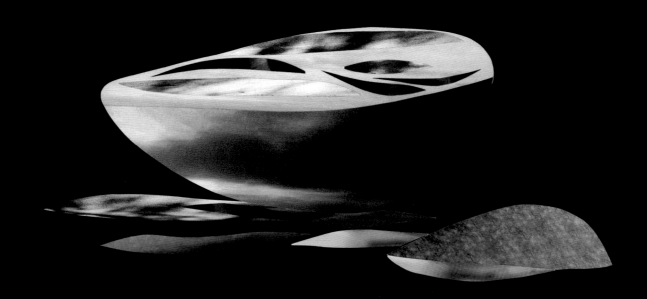

A PIQUANT *MESCLUN* SALAD *with* ORANGE CONFITS AND SOY SAUCE

SERVES 4, 25 MINS

about 125 g (4½ oz) *mesclun* salad

1 whole orange

juice of 1 orange

4 tbls soy sauce, either a regular, light or salt-reduced version, according to taste

1 tbls raspberry vinegar

1 tbls caster sugar (superfine sugar)

8 tbls virgin olive oil

½ tsp fine-grained, creamy-textured mustard, ideally *moutarde d'Orléans*

about 100 g (4 oz) shavings of fresh Parmesan

freshly ground black pepper

DRINK WITH

A young white Sancerre

SERVE WITH

Bread of your choice, served warm or toasted

Orange and soy sauce? Yes, together they can make an excellent seasoning for a salad! More precisely, what we have here is a garnish of orange *confits*, with soy sauce incorporated into the *confit* syrup. The blend of two flavours reminds me of the piquant edge of a chilli pepper. It's a racy garnish for the excellent assortment of tender young leaves which characterizes *mesclun* salad. There is nothing like it to give a little kick to your menu. If you are a meat-eater, it is particularly well suited to partnering smoked duck breast. You might even use it to replace your cheeseboard after a main course.

———————————

To make the orange *confits*, use a mandolin or an extremely sharp knife to slice the whole orange into very fine rounds; remove the pips. Choose a sauté pan, preferably with flared sides, which will accommodate the slices spread out in a single layer. Arrange them in the pan, then cover with the orange juice, soy sauce, raspberry vinegar, sugar and 8 turns of a mill of black pepper.

Simmer the ingredients over low heat, turning the slices of orange occasionally, until their peel and membrane become tender and all of the liquid has evaporated.

In the bottom of a large salad bowl, whisk together the mustard and the olive oil vigorously to form a smooth, homogeneous dressing. Add the *mesclun* salad leaves and the slices of orange *confits*, and toss them gently, to coat them evenly in the dressing. Taste and adjust seasoning if needed. Scatter over shavings of fresh Parmesan and serve with the bread or toast of your choice.

RED ARROCHA *with* RHUBARB, BEETROOT AND BAY

SERVES 4, 1 HR 20 MINS

2–4 handfuls of red arrocha leaves
or baby spinach leaves, washed,
and ribs removed

2 sticks of rhubarb

about 4 baby beetroots (beets) or
2 larger ones, uncooked

2 fresh bay leaves

100 g (4 oz) lightly salted butter

1 tbls caster sugar (superfine sugar)

1 tbls virgin olive oil

fleur de sel or salt of your choice

DRINK WITH

A dry white from the Jurançon region,
preferably a Collioure Blanc

For me this dish is an absolute picture, like a chalk drawing with wonderful hues of reddish brown. The magnificent colour is largely to do with the leaves of red arrocha, which comes from the same family as spinach, and ranks as one of Europe's oldest vegetables. I find the recent revival of interest in its colour and flavour more than justified. To charm the arrocha into showing off its culinary attributes, I have introduced it here to three other delights from the garden: rhubarb, bay and beetroot. During cooking, the arrocha releases little beads of translucent, ruby-tinted juice which merge beautifully with the juices of the rhubarb and beetroot. It is a little out of the ordinary for arrocha, whose silky leaves are often used raw in salads, but it works. Since spinach is a cousin of red arrocha, you can use it as a substitute.

———————————

Cook the beetroots, covered, in lightly salted simmering water for 30–60 minutes, depending on size. Drain them and, when cool enough to handle, peel off their skins. Leave baby beetroots whole. Cut any larger ones into the shapes of your choice.

Put the butter, the 2 whole sticks of rhubarb, the sugar and the bay leaves into a wide sauté pan with flared sides or into a saucepan. Add enough cold water to barely cover the ingredients and simmer, partially covered, for about 12 minutes. Turn the rhubarb over, add the beetroot and continue to simmer gently for a further 15 minutes or until the rhubarb is lightly caramelized.

Add the red arrocha and stir it around the bottom of the pan until, after a few minutes, the leaves have flopped slightly. Season to taste with salt; add a swirl of olive oil. Cut the sticks of rhubarb in half, arrange the assembly on four warm table plates and serve without delay.

SPINACH AND CARROTS
with ORANGE AND SESAME

SERVES 4, 1 HR

750 g (2 lb) fresh spinach leaves, central ribs removed and the leaves washed

2 bunches of new baby carrots, weighing about 1 kg (2.2 lb) in total, their leaves cut back to leave a little stalk in place; the carrots washed and left in their skin

juice of 5 oranges

2 tbls white sesame seeds, toasted for a few minutes in a non-stick frying pan

30 g (1 oz/2 tbls) caster sugar (superfine sugar)

juice of 1 lemon

1 large lemon, very finely sliced into rounds, pips removed

75 g (3 oz /6 tbls) lightly salted butter, preferably clarified

freshly grated nutmeg

a splash of sesame oil

fleur de sel or salt of your choice

DRINK WITH

A young Riesling from Alsace or a Sauvignon from the Loire

Here you can expect flamboyance and a riot of flavours and colours: from the citrus family, an interesting duel between the sharpness of the lemon and the sweetness of the orange; and from our vegetable gardens, the appearance of two firm favourites: spinach and carrots. And what comes out of it all? Something mouth-watering which brings taste buds to life. Against a background of interwoven flavours, the final garnish of toasted sesame seeds completes an interplay of taste and texture, and gives the dish a remarkably long-lasting flavour.

Put the sugar into a heavy based saucepan and pour over the lemon juice. Lay the slices of lemon on top and set the saucepan over very low heat. Leave the mixture without stirring, for 10–12 minutes or until the slices are translucent, syrupy, and transformed into *confits*.

Meanwhile, arrange the carrots so that they lie flat in a large sauté pan, preferably with flared sides. Add the orange juice, along with about one-third of the butter, and simmer the ingredients until the carrots are tender and the orange juice has reduced and blended with the butter to form a glaze. If the liquid evaporates before the carrots are cooked, add a little water.

To cook the spinach, set a large saucepan over low heat, and add half of the remaining butter together with half of the washed spinach with the water that clings to its leaves. Turn the spinach gently for a couple of minutes or until the water has evaporated. Remove from the heat. Add the remaining butter to the bottom of the pan and cook the remaining spinach, rapidly over medium heat, for a minute or so, or until the leaves have flopped and the butter acquires a slightly nutty aroma. Transfer the spinach to a colander for several minutes, then arrange it on a warm serving dish.

Add the hot carrots lightly coated with the orange and butter glaze. Sprinkle with salt, freshly grated nutmeg and the toasted sesame seeds. Drizzle over 2 ribbons of sesame oil and serve with the lemon *confits*.

STAND
UP
ASPARAGUS

SERVES 4, 1 HR 50 MINS

24 thick or jumbo asparagus spears about
1.5 cm (⅝ inch) diameter

100 g (4 oz/8 tbls) lightly salted butter, clarified

4 eggs

leaves from a small bunch of chervil (optional)

fleur de sel or salt of your choice

DRINK WITH

A white wine from Alsace, preferably a Pinot Blanc,
a Chasselas or a dry Muscat

In terms of culinary technique, this is an exhibition piece. The idea is to gather asparagus into a bundle using greaseproof (waxed) paper, then cook it vertically in a deep saucepan. During the cooking process, heat is directed mainly to the stalks of the asparagus at the base of the pan while the tips are basted occasionally with spoonfuls of hot melted butter. The tender tips will emerge barely cooked, while the firm stalks will be tenderized and the middle sections will retain some bite. A key to success is the pan itself, which should be 12–15 cm (4¾–6 inches) high and at least 20 cm (8 inches) in diameter, to allow the circulation of heat around the bundled spears.

————————————

Choose only the freshest possible asparagus with tightly closed tips and firm stalks, free of cracks. Cut away any woody stalk or tough ends and trim to a uniform length. Rinse the spears in cold water and drain on a kitchen towel. To bundle up the asparagus for cooking, make a band of double greaseproof paper wide enough to wrap the spears comfortably; it should be tall enough to cover the spears to three-quarters of their height. Lay the band on the counter and place the spears on top, with their stalk-ends neatly lined up with the bottom edge. Wrap the spears in the paper, then secure with several rounds of kitchen string, tying it – not too tightly – towards the top.

Put the clarified butter in the bottom of a suitably narrow deep asparagus pan, then add the spears, standing on their stalks, and cook them over the lowest possible heat for up to 90 minutes, taking care not to let the butter cook beyond a delicious nutty stage. For thicker spears and for white asparagus the time can increase to 2 or 2½ hours. When ready, the base should be soft, the middle firm and the tips crunchy. During this time, baste the tips every 20 minutes or so with spoonfuls of butter from the bottom of the pan.

Just before serving, poach the eggs for about 6 minutes; transfer them to a warm serving dish. Present the bundled asparagus on a separate dish, cutting the string and removing the paper at the table. If you like, scatter with chopped chervil. Transfer the asparagus-flavoured cooking butter to a sauce-boat. Serve each guest with about 6 spears and one egg. Offer *fleur de sel* and, above all, the buttery sauce.

ASPARAGUS AND PEAR *with* A TOUCH OF RED SORREL

SERVES 4, 40 MINS

8 jumbo asparagus spears, trimmed and peeled free of any tough woody stalks

1 large ripe pear, preferably a Comice, Williams or Beurré Hardy, cut into 8 segments, cored, with the skin left intact

1 large bunch of red sorrel (or green sorrel if red is unavailable)

50 g (2 oz) lightly salted butter

½ lemon

fleur de sel or salt of your choice

freshly ground black pepper

DRINK WITH

A young Riesling from Alsace

Asparagus and pear – two types of ivory-coloured flesh offering you a merry dance of flavour, ushered along by red sorrel. Acting as a catalyst, the sorrel's fruity acidity makes the duo throb with life. When the sorrel's ruby-coloured juices are released by cooking onto the asparagus and pear, it's a sight to behold, an authentic still-life painting.

Blanch the asparagus spears in lightly salted simmering water for about 4 minutes. Drain them, rinse in cold water to arrest their cooking, then drain again, taking care to avoid damaging their tips. Lay them on a kitchen towel to dry.

In a large frying pan, or skillet, set over gentle heat, melt the butter and, when it foams very lightly, add the spears and turn them in the butter for about 15 minutes. Add the segments of pear and turn them carefully at intervals until lightly and evenly coloured (about 5 minutes). Add the sorrel leaves, and when they have wilted after a few minutes, distribute them between the segments of pear and the asparagus spears.

Arrange the ingredients elegantly on a warm serving dish. Add the lemon juice to the buttery deposits in the pan and stir together to make a sauce. Drizzle this lemon butter sauce over the assembly, then season with salt and freshly ground black pepper. Serve individual portions at the table. The vibrant combination of flavours is best appreciated in mouthfuls made up of half a segment of pear, half an asparagus spear and a morsel of the red sorrel to lend a note of sharpness. A lively treat indeed.

BABY TURNIPS *with* LEMON AND BLACK PEPPER

SERVES 4, 30 MINS

2 bunches of baby turnips of an even size, weighing about 900 g (2 lb), washed, with stalks left intact

80 g (3 oz) lightly salted butter

leaves from ½ bunch of basil

1 large lemon, thinly sliced preferably using a mandolin, pips removed

1 heaped tbls caster sugar (superfine sugar)

fleur de sel or salt of your choice

freshly ground black pepper

DRINK WITH

A white wine from Corsica, preferably a Vermentino

SERVE WITH

A *mesclun* salad tossed in virgin olive oil

I've always had a soft spot for baby turnips. It is their subtle hint of bitterness which intrigues me, along with their understated elegance. I had the idea of confronting them with a mighty burst of flavour from basil and lemon *confits*: these little darlings of today's master chefs show their true colours and stand up valiantly to the challenge. Here, the aromatic confrontation is accentuated by the smoky edge of the black pepper.

———————————

Arrange the turnips in a single layer in a sauté pan, preferably with flared sides. Add the butter and enough water to immerse the turnips to half their depth. Put a round of greaseproof (waxed) paper on top and cook the turnips over gentle heat until the water has evaporated and the turnips are tender.

Meanwhile, make the lemon *confits*: put the sugar in a small, heavy based saucepan and add enough water to just cover it – about 4 tablespoons. Lay the slices of lemon on top. Add half of the basil leaves, tearing any large ones. Cover the saucepan with a lid and cook over very low heat for 10 minutes, or until the slices of lemon are transformed by the syrup into tender, translucent *confits*. During this time, remove the lid every 3 minutes or so to check that the mixture is neither cooking too quickly nor sticking to the bottom of the pan. If it is, add a little more water.

When the turnips are tender, add the remaining basil leaves and glaze the turnips in the buttery juices from the bottom of the pan. Season with salt and freshly ground black pepper. Arrange the turnips on a warm serving dish and decorate with the lemon *confits* draped in basil. As an accompaniment, a *mesclun* salad will mediate nicely between the turnips and the *confits*.

PEAS AND PINK GRAPEFRUIT
with WHITE ALMONDS

SERVES 4, 35 MINS

about 350 g (12½ oz) fresh garden peas (*petits pois*), shelled

1 pink grapefruit

16–20 blanched almonds left whole or cut in halves or quarters lengthways

40 g (1½ oz) lightly salted butter

2 tbls virgin olive oil

flowers from 2 small sprigs of fresh thyme

fleur de sel or salt of your choice

DRINK WITH

A Sancerre or a Sauvignon Blanc from the Loire

Here, we are in a situation approaching fantasy. Certainly, when we bring together garden peas and pink grapefruit, we verge on culinary improbability. Yet, in agreeing to a rendezvous, the two accomplices lead us to an unexpected pleasure garden, heavy with the scent of fresh thyme. The addition of almonds offsets the slightly astringent note of this partnership, and offers some deliciously playful bite.

_____

Peel the grapefruit, removing as much of the pith and core as possible. With a small sharp knife, free the grapefruit segments by cutting along the sections of membrane and letting the segments and juices fall away on to a plate. Cut the segments into bite-sized pieces and set them aside.

In a sauté pan with sloping sides, or in a saucepan, melt the butter and the olive oil over low heat. Stir in the fresh thyme flowers and garden peas. Cover with water to a depth of about 4 cm (1½ inches). Simmer the peas, stirring frequently, for about 11 minutes or until the water evaporates and the peas are cooked to an *al dente* stage.

Meanwhile, have ready 4 warm soup bowls and the almonds: you can leave the almonds whole or, if you prefer, cut them lengthways into halves or quarters. Season the cooked peas with salt and discard the thyme flowers. Divide the peas between the soup bowls. Arrange the grapefruit segments on top, distribute the almonds and serve straight away.

PASSION FRUIT, STUFFED AND BAKED LIKE A CRUMBLE

SERVES 4, 55 MINS PLUS 30 MINS COOLING

4 passion fruits

15 g (½ oz) lightly salted butter

1 apple, peeled, cored and diced

30 g (1 oz) light brown soft sugar

10 g (½ oz) caster sugar (superfine sugar)

leaves from 6 sprigs of basil, finely chopped

40 g (1½ oz) raspberry jam

a pinch of cinnamon

½ vanilla pod (bean), split and the seeds scraped out or split and very finely chopped

30 g (1 oz) toasted slivered almonds

20 g (¾ oz) ground almonds

icing sugar (confectioner's sugar) to serve

DRINK WITH

A young white wine: a Gewurztraminer Vendages Tardives (VD) or a sweet Chenin Blanc (Chenin Moelleux) from the Loire.

I'm mad about these little passion fruits. Their flesh is scooped out and mixed with sweet delicacies, then returned to the emptied shells and baked.

I am only too delighted to use the shells in this way because they make such ideal containers. I eat the filling from the shell with a little spoon just like a boiled egg and it makes a charming dessert. In this recipe, a sprinkling of ground almonds and brown sugar adds a crunchy crust like a crumble.

————————————

To make the basis for the filling: melt the butter in a sauté pan set over low heat, and add the apple, half of the brown sugar, all of the white caster sugar, the basil, jam, cinnamon and vanilla. Stir for a few minutes to ensure the ingredients have melded together yet retain some crunch. Set this mixture aside briefly.

Cut the passion fruits in half. Using a tea or coffee spoon, scrape out the flesh and stir it into the reserved mixture, keeping the empty shells. Stir the toasted slivered almonds into the mixture to complete the filling. Taste it and add more sugar if desired. Spoon the filling into the shells, piling it into little domes. Mix the remaining brown sugar with the ground almonds and sprinkle this combination over each filled shell.

Put a few drops of water in the bottom of a shallow baking dish, add the shells and transfer the dish to an oven preheated to 180°C (350°F, Gas Mark 4). Bake for 30 minutes.

Remove the fruits from the oven and leave them to relax and cool for about 30 minutes. Serve them with a fine sprinkling of icing sugar.

A SUMMER GARDEN OF VEGETABLES GARNISHED WITH TURNIP LEAVES

SERVES 4, 1 HR 15 MINS

turnip leaves from 4 mauve turnips

2 beetroots (beets), either red, yellow or white

4 yellow or purple carrots, or whatever colour you prefer

4 orange carrots

4 small black radishes

2 tbls white wine vinegar

70 g (3 oz) acacia honey or pale runny honey of your choice

150 ml (¾ US cup) peanut or groundnut oil

½ cucumber, peeled free of any thick skin, then cut lengthways and scraped free of its watery seeds

1 courgette (zucchini), peeled free of any thick skin

2 tomatoes, preferably Noir de Crimée

4 red radishes, washed, a little of their green stalk intact

a few handfuls of *mesclun* salad

DRINK WITH

A dry Chenin Blanc from the Loire, preferably a Vouvray or a Jasnières

TO SERVE AS A MAIN COURSE

Increase the quantities of some or all of the vegetables, as well as the salad. Offer the dish with olive or nut bread, or the bread of your choice.

A great classic from the kitchen of L'Arpege, essentially a splendid crop of colourful vegetables prepared simply, and with total respect for their natural beauty. Some are cooked; others remain raw. The blanched turnip leaves can be incorporated into the accompanying salad or offered separately for diners to use them as wraps for little mouthfuls of vegetables. The dressing, which includes white wine vinegar and honey, is designed to bring out the essential flavours of the produce. I adore the contrast here between sweet and sour, and I like the artful play between cooked and raw. For best effect, choose vegetables of a small to medium size. At the restaurant, I like to present the vegetables heaped into a dome.

In separate saucepans, cook the beetroots, carrots and black radishes – in their skins – in lightly salted water, to an *al dente* stage. Leave them to cool in their cooking water. Peel the beetroots and carrots. Leave the skin of the black radishes intact. Set these vegetables aside.

Cut the turnip leaves to make about 16 leaf-shaped wraps for the vegetables. Blanch them in lightly salted water for 3–4 seconds, refresh them in iced water to arrest their cooking, then drain on a kitchen towel.

In a bowl, mix or whisk the vinegar and honey together until well blended. Incorporate the peanut oil in small trickles, stirring continuously – as you would if making a mayonnaise – until you have a homogenous dressing of coating consistency; set aside in a sauce-boat.

Create a dome-shaped assembly of the cooked and uncooked vegetables: leave small specimens of beetroots and carrots whole and cut larger ones how you like. Cut the black radishes into large dice or batons. Cut the cucumber and courgette into the shapes of your choice and add them to the assembly along with the quartered tomatoes. Distribute the red radishes – which usually look good left whole. Garnish with the petal-shaped turnip leaves and surround with some *mesclun* salad. Serve with the dressing on the side.

GLOBE ARTICHOKES *with* BAY LEAVES AND LIME

You will need no more than an artful turn of the hand for this recipe. You simply tuck bay leaves between the leaves of an uncooked artichoke to multiply the flavours and scents while it cooks. Once the artichoke is cooked, you only have to peel back the first few leaves to get the overwhelming effect. The artichoke is a secretive little thing, and the best is yet to come: the sublime heart awaits.

SERVES 4, 1 HR 50 MINS PLUS 1 HR COOLING

4 large globe artichokes with tightly packed leaves

12 large fresh bay leaves

6–8 tbls virgin olive oil

juice of 1 lime

fleur de sel or salt of your choice

DRINK WITH

A Gewurztraminer from Alsace, Sélection de Grains Nobles (SGN)

SERVE WITH

Toasted wholemeal bread

Trim back the stalks of the artichokes. Cut the bay leaves in half lengthways. Tuck the bay leaves into the artichoke leaves, distributing them evenly and hiding them well. Wrap each artichoke in several rounds of cling film (Saran wrap).

Fill a deep stock-pot, or deep saucepan, half-full with unsalted water and bring it to a boil. Meanwhile, have ready a saucepan lid which is slightly smaller than the stock-pot and, also, some small weights. Lower the artichokes into the boiling water. Allow them to float, and then submerge them with the saucepan lid held in place by the weights. Simmer the artichokes for 1½ hours. During this time add more water to the pan if it evaporates.

Remove the artichokes from the water with a slotted spoon and leave them to cool for one hour in their cling film. Meanwhile, make a dressing by mixing together the olive oil and the lime juice. Put this in a sauce-boat and set it aside.

To serve, unwrap the artichokes and arrange them on 4 table plates, adding a small mound of quality sea-salt at the side of each. Toasted wholemeal bread makes a perfect accompaniment for the inimitable artichoke hearts.

HARICOTS VERTS *with* WHITE PEACH AND WHITE ALMONDS

SERVES 4, 20 MINS

600 g (1 lb 5 oz) haricots verts, extra fine

1 large white peach, stoned and cut into 12 segments

12 whole blanched almonds, cut in half lengthways if desired

40 g (1½ oz) lightly salted butter

a long dash of virgin olive oil

a few purple basil leaves, or green if purple basil is unavailable

fleur de sel or salt of your choice

freshly ground black pepper

DRINK WITH

A Condrieu or a full-bodied white made with the Viognier grape

For me, the peach is nature's own summer sorbet: its fresh clear juice, with the scent of white flowers, has a sweetness that never cloys; its soft flesh melts in the mouth. Put the peach with haricots verts and you have a fine marriage of textures and flavours. Add almonds, and you have an arousing contrast and a fabulous note of crunch.

———————————

Plunge the haricots verts into lightly salted boiling water. Return to the boil, then cook, uncovered, to *al dente* stage – usually 2–3 minutes for extra fine beans. Drain them, immerse in cold water to arrest their cooking and preserve colour, then drain again.

In a large sauté pan set over low heat, melt the butter and a long dash of olive oil. Add the haricots verts, shaking the pan to coat them, then add the almonds, segments of peach and basil leaves. Leave these ingredients to warm through gently – but do not stir them or they may lose their fragile shape and beauty. Season with salt and freshly ground black pepper. Arrange the assembly on 4 warm table plates and eat straight away.

TURNIPS AND NEW POTATOES
with RED TOMATOES

SERVES 4, 45 MINS

a bunch of baby turnips on their stalks weighing about 450 g (1 lb)

12 small new potatoes in their skins, washed

4 large 'beefsteak' tomatoes, cored, skinned, deseeded and cut into segments

4 tbls virgin olive oil

leaves from 2 sprigs of tarragon

40 g (1½ oz) lightly salted butter

fleur de sel or salt of your choice

freshly ground black pepper

DRINK WITH

A dry white Bordeaux, like Entre-Deux-Mers; alternatively, a dry white Bergerac

TO SERVE AS A MAIN COURSE

Increase the quantities of some or all of the vegetables and make a larger batch of tomato coulis. Serve with wild rice, a green salad and warm tomato bread.

This trio of vegetables is a little out of the ordinary but nevertheless delicious. A harmonious chord is struck, as the bitterness of the turnip is balanced by the sweet succulence of the tomato and the mild roundedness of potato. The distinctive note of anise from the tarragon pushes the register of flavour into a contemporary key.

————————————

In a sauté pan with flared sides, cook the tomatoes in 2 tablespoons of the olive oil over brisk heat: toss the mixture over high heat for a minute or two, then lower the heat slightly and stir regularly until the liquid has evaporated and the tomatoes have reduced to a thick coulis.

Meanwhile, put the turnips and potatoes into a saucepan with enough cold water to barely cover them. Add the remaining olive oil. Simmer over gentle heat until the water evaporates, then turn the vegetables just long enough to give them a little colour.

To serve the dish, stir the tarragon into the reduced tomato coulis, season it with salt and transfer it to a warm serving dish. Finish the turnips and potatoes by adding the butter and turning them in it until they are glazed. Adjust seasoning with salt and freshly ground black pepper. Arrange the vegetables on top of the tomato coulis and serve straight away.

MELON *with* BLUE CHEESE AND BLACK PEPPER

SERVES 4, 40 MINS

1 large ripe melon

150–200 g (5–7 oz) *fourme d'Ambert*, or Stilton

3–4 tbls virgin olive oil

several handfuls of red or green sorrel, washed, and tough ribs removed

leaves from a bunch of purple or green basil

1 tbls balsamic vinegar

fleur de sel or salt of your choice

1 tbls black peppercorns crushed or coarsely ground

DRINK WITH
A Pineau de Charentes or a Floc de Gascogne

The blue vein, creamy-textured cheese I use for this dish is *fourme d'Ambert*. If this is difficult for you to source outside of France, you could replace it with Stilton. The cheese is combined with sweet, fully ripe melon – which is lightly sautéed – to make one of the tastiest *chaud-froid* dishes I know. As an accompaniment, a salad of red sorrel and purple basil offers some arresting colour as well as a delicate astringency, but you could equally well use green varieties of both. Black pepper supports the whole dish.

————————

Cut the cheese into four equal-sized portions and leave them at room temperature for about half an hour.

Meanwhile, cut the melon into quarters, and scoop out and discard the seeds. Thinly cover the bottom of a sauté pan with about one tablespoon of the olive oil, holding back the rest; arrange the melon quarters, flat on their side, in a single layer, in the pan. Partially cover with a lid and stew the melon quarters gently over low heat for 25 minutes, turning them over from time to time.

While the melon is stewing gently, put the leaves of sorrel and basil in a salad bowl and dress them gently with the remaining olive oil.

To serve, arrange a quarter of melon, a portion of cheese and a helping of the salad on 4 individual plates. Season to taste with salt and coarsely crushed or ground black pepper. Sign each plate with a trail of balsamic vinegar.

NEW POTATOES
with SAGE

SERVES 4, 30 MINS

about 900 g (2 lb) even-sized new potatoes
(allow about 4 potatoes per person)

leaves from 4 sprigs of fresh sage

1 small head of new garlic, split lengthways into 4,
roughly peeled

50 g (2 oz) lightly salted butter, preferably clarified

fleur de sel or salt of your choice

DRINK WITH

A red Bandol made with Mourvèdre grapes

Sage has long been a source of inspiration to me. It is perhaps surprising to learn how much it can flatter new potatoes. You use sage leaves in much the same way as you would fresh bay leaves in many classical recipes. The difference is that sage offers more refinement. Its mild astringency will lift the mild, fluffy flesh of the new potato, and its scent will lift your spirits as well. In this recipe, the little touch of garlic at the end of cooking rounds off flavours and lends a warm reminder of traditional potato dishes from the past.

_____

Put the butter in a heat-proof casserole, or Dutch oven – preferably made of enamelled cast iron – and set it over gentle heat. Add the sage leaves and when they soften slightly – after a minute or so – add the split garlic and let it soften for 15–20 minutes without colouring. During this time, the butter should murmur very gently without burning.

Meanwhile, cook the potatoes in their skins, in a separate saucepan, in gently simmering salted water. Test after about 10 minutes – the potatoes should be cooked *au point* and retain a little resistance; drain.

Spoon the potatoes gently into the flavoured butter in the casserole, and leave them to colour gently, and continue cooking, for several minutes. Season with salt. Serve the potatoes, garnished with the sage leaves, either as a first course or as an accompaniment for roast guinea fowl.
A simple but very pleasant treat.

RATATOUILLE BRITTANY-STYLE IN BUTTER

**SERVES 4, 1 HR PLUS
30 MINS COOLING**

100 g (4 oz) salted butter, preferably from Brittany, clarified

1 large sweet onion, such as a Spanish or Roscoff onion, finely sliced

4 large tomatoes, preferably 1 red, 1 black or bronze, 1 yellow and 1 orange, all cored, skinned, deseeded and cut into large segments or quarters

1 small head of new garlic, peeled and crushed

2 large firm courgettes (zucchini), one cut into batons, the other cut into very fine rounds

1 large aubergine (eggplant)

1 red pepper

1 green pepper

leaves from a small bunch of basil

a few splashes of virgin olive oil

a few dashes of soy sauce to taste

fleur de sel or salt of your choice

DRINK WITH

A Crozes-Hermitage or a Saint-Joseph

TO SERVE AS A MAIN COURSE

Double the portion size and serve with either couscous or quinoa or, better still, a mixture of quinoa and bulgar – which can be bought as a ready-mix in many supermarkets. Olive bread is an excellent choice to offer with this dish.

I enjoy taking this legendary dish of Provence to Brittany, where instead of olive oil the cooks prefer to exploit the wonders of their local salted butter. The butter's assertive personality has much to offer this dish. In particular, its distinctive saltiness gets the seasoning off to a good start and throws flavours into relief. The recipe combines cooked and uncooked vegetables, for a nice interplay of temperatures as well as textures.

————————

In a large sauté pan – preferably with flared sides – sweat the onion in two-thirds of the butter over very gentle heat until it softens slightly. Add half the quantity of the tomatoes, the garlic and the courgette cut into batons. Partially cover the pan with a lid and leave the ingredients to stew very gently for about 40 minutes, or until the watery juices from the tomatoes have evaporated.

Meanwhile, blister the skin of the peppers, as well as the aubergine, to make it easy to peel away their skin. The best way to do this is to skewer each vegetable whole and pass it through a naked flame from a gas hob or an open fire. If this is impractical, then use a regular grill. To make the blistered peppers easy to peel, wrap them briefly in a kitchen towel wrung out in cold water. Peel them, cut them into strips and add them to the simmering ratatouille mixture.

When the aubergine is sufficiently blistered, leave it to cool for up to 30 minutes, then spoon out its flesh and put it in a saucepan along with the remaining butter. Stir to blend over low to medium heat until the pulp is lightly coloured; season with salt and set aside in a warm place.

Prepare the uncooked ingredients for presentation: put the remaining tomatoes and courgette in a salad bowl along with the basil. Dress the ingredients with olive oil blended with a few drops of soy sauce to taste; set this aside at room temperature.

To serve, season the hot ratatouille with a few drops of soy sauce to taste, and transfer it to a large, warm serving dish. You can add the aubergine pulp to this dish or present it separately in a warm sauce boat. Offer the salad bowl of uncooked vegetables separately. Let diners help themselves and enjoy the elements of hot and cold.

THREE KINDS OF TOMATOES *with* ROASTED AUBERGINE (EGGPLANT) CAVIAR

SERVES 4, 35 MINS PLUS 20 MINS COOLING

2 red tomatoes, cored, and peeled if desired

2 white tomatoes, cored, and peeled if desired

2 yellow tomatoes, cored, and peeled if desired

2 large aubergines (eggplants)

leaves from ½ bunch of purple basil, or green basil if purple is unavailable

8 tbls virgin olive oil

juice of ½ lemon

fleur de sel or salt of your choice

freshly ground black pepper

DRINK WITH

A red from the Languedoc such as a Faugères, or a Pic Saint-Loup or a Minervois

The key to this simple yet delicious recipe is to burn the skin of the aubergines to impart a lovely smoky flavour to their flesh. The ideal way to do this is to put each one on a long skewer – or pinch it with some pliers – and then turn it in the naked flame of a gas hob or an open fire. If this is not practical, you can grill the aubergines – cut in half if you like – or you can roast them whole in the oven, albeit with a slight loss of the smoky flavour. We refer to the roasted aubergine flesh as 'caviar' partly because the flesh carries little pockets of seeds recalling the eggs of sturgeon, and partly because it is a great delicacy. Fully ripe tomatoes, preferably a mixture of colours, will be only too delighted to find themselves in such exquisite company.

―――――――――――

Burn the skins of the aubergines either by passing them through a flame or by grilling them for 15–20 minutes. Alternatively, you can roast them in a medium oven for up to an hour. Once the skins have blistered sufficiently, leave the aubergines to cool for about 20 minutes.

Meanwhile, cut the tomatoes into segments and deseed them. Arrange them on 4 table plates. Drizzle over half the quantity of olive oil and season the tomatoes to taste. When the aubergines are cool enough to handle – but still warm – use a small sharp knife to cut and loosen their skin, then spoon out the 'caviar' flesh carefully and transfer it to a bowl. Beat it lightly with a fork and gradually incorporate the rest of the olive oil and the lemon juice. Taste it and adjust seasoning. Spoon it on to the plates and decorate with the basil leaves. Serve the dish, while the caviar is still warm, with the toast of your choice.

TOMATOES AND MOZZARELLA
with VANILLA AND MINT

SERVES 4, 25 MINS PLUS UP TO 1 HR FOR MACERATION OF DRESSING

4 large ripe tomatoes, peeled and cored

2 balls of buffalo mozzarella

¼ vanilla pod (bean) split open

leaves from 4–6 sprigs of fresh mint

200 ml (14 tbls/⅞ US cup) virgin olive oil

finely grated zest of ½ lemon

several handfuls of mixed salad leaves, preferably a combination of *mesclun* and rocket

12 whole blanched almonds, cut lengthways into halves or splinters

a dash of balsamic vinegar

fleur de sel or salt of your choice

freshly ground pepper of your choice

DRINK WITH

A Vermentino from Provence

With perfectly ripe, good quality tomatoes – perhaps from your own garden – this salad is a great delicacy, its sweetness warranting the status of a dessert. The secret? A tomato with some sunshine inside.

———————————

Start by making the dressing: in a bowl, combine the olive oil, the lemon zest, the split vanilla pod and the mint leaves. Leave these ingredients to macerate for up to one hour.

Cut the tomatoes in half lengthways, deseed them, and cut the halves into fairly thick slices. Cut the balls of mozzarella into similar slices. Arrange all of the slices so that they alternate and overlap slightly, on 4 table plates. Surround the arrangement with salad leaves and scatter with the almonds, leaving a small margin free along one side of the plate.

Strain the dressing – discarding the solids – and spoon it over the assembly. Drizzle a thin trail of balsamic vinegar along the margin. Season with salt and a few fresh grindings of pepper, and serve.

CAESAR SALAD

SERVES 4, 30 MINS

4 small even-sized (preferably waxy) potatoes in their skin, scrubbed

2 large eggs

4 tomatoes, preferably a so-called 'black' variety such as Noir de Crimée, Marmande, Black Prince or Black Krim

1 or 2 romaine or cos lettuces, or several hearts, washed, dried and torn into bite-sized pieces

about 2 tbls coarsely chopped herbs including chervil, coriander (cilantro) and basil

1 large red onion, preferably a Red Brunswick, finely sliced

12 small fresh filleted anchovies, or 12 preserved anchovies rinsed free of salt

1 tsp fine-grained, creamy-textured mustard, ideally *moutarde d'Orléans*

8 tbls virgin olive oil

shavings of fresh Parmesan

fleur de sel or salt of your choice

freshly ground white pepper

DRINK WITH

A dry white Spanish wine or a chilled dry *fino* sherry

TO SERVE AS A MAIN COURSE

Increase or double the portion size. Serve with farmhouse or olive bread, rubbed with a clove of crushed garlic, and toasted.

This is my own little Caesar salad. I adore making it because I enjoy the complex range of ingredients. By varying the quantities, I am able to achieve a different texture and flavour each time I make it. Enjoy yourself with this game of variation. You can also experiment with the salad's seasonings: mustard, Parmesan, pepper, fresh herbs, even the *fleur de sel*. In fact, I have sometimes replaced *fleur de sel* from Guérande with a light soy sauce.

―――――――――――――――

Cook the potatoes, partially covered, in lightly simmering salted water until they are tender – about 12–20 minutes depending on size. Drain them and, when they are cool enough to handle, cut them into slices. Put the eggs into simmering water, then let the water return to a light boil and cook them until firmly set but not dry – about 6–7 minutes. Plunge the eggs into cold water briefly to arrest their cooking, then peel them and cut them in half. Core the tomatoes, peel them if desired, then cut them in quarters and deseed them.

In a large salad bowl, combine the lettuce, herbs, onion, tomatoes, potatoes and anchovies. Whisk together the mustard and the olive oil until well blended and drizzle this dressing over the salad ingredients. Use salad servers to lift and coat the salad gently in the dressing.

Present the salad on individual table plates, adding half a boiled egg and a few shavings of fresh Parmesan to each one. Season with salt and freshly ground white pepper.

WHITE CHILLI
THE WAY I LIKE IT

SERVES 4, 1 HR 15 MINS
PLUS 25 MINS RESTING

250 g (9 oz) haricots
blancs, preferably Cocos
de Paimpol, in their pods,
or about 125 g (4½ oz/½
US cup) dried haricot (navy)
beans soaked overnight
and rinsed

about 40 g (1½ oz/3 tbls)
salted butter

3 white tomatoes, small to
medium size, cored, skinned,
deseeded and cut into large
segments or quarters

2 small bulbs of fennel,
cut in half lengthways

1 large white carrot or about
100 g (4 oz) celeriac, peeled
and cut into thick segments

1 chilli pepper, red or
green, deseeded and
finely chopped

1 stick of white celery,
cut into bite sized segments

3 cloves of new garlic,
peeled and crushed

3 shallots, peeled and finely
chopped

3 white onions, weighing
about 100 g (4 oz), peeled
and finely chopped

350 ml (11 fl oz/1½ US cups)
whole milk

a few flowers of fresh thyme

fleur de sel or salt of
your choice

DRINK WITH
A red Chateauneuf-du-Pape

TO SERVE AS A MAIN COURSE
Increase or double the portion size and serve with black,
red or white tagliatelle

I took great pleasure in creating this variation of chilli and beans. My aim was to confine the composition to shades of white. Once I had decided to experiment with it, my eye guided my hands when they picked the vegetables from the garden. And so it was that the ingredients – originally including varieties of white carrot and yellowish white tomato – fell into the saucepan of their own accord. When white carrot is hard to source you can replace it with celeriac. Amongst the various varieties of white tomatoes available today, the White Tomesol is the whitest while the Great White is a yellowish-white beefsteak tomato.

This recipe is a great first course, as well as a superb accompaniment to certain main courses, especially pan-fried cod. In a larger quantity, the dish might become a main course in its own right, accompanied by a salad and served with black, red or white tagliatelle. I have fond memories of taking this white chilli dish to the table for the first time, and sharing it with fellow chefs. It was a well-received debut.

———————————

Melt the butter in a large saucepan set over low heat. Add the haricots blancs, tomatoes, fennel, carrot or celeriac, chilli pepper, celery, garlic, shallots, onions and the milk; cover with a lid set askew. Adjust the heat to maintain a light simmer, with the milk murmuring gently without boiling, for 50 minutes. During this time, add a small cup of cold milk if the liquid overheats or reduces too quickly.

Leave the ingredients to cool and relax for 25 minutes. Return the saucepan to the heat to warm through the ingredients briefly, and then adjust seasoning with salt. Arrange on warm individual plates, adding a garnish of thyme flowers and a delicate trail of virgin olive oil to each helping.

PEACHES *with* LEMON AND SAFFRON

SERVES 4, 40 MINS

4 yellow peaches, each one stoned and cut into
6 segments with the skin intact

1 lemon, cut into 6 segments, pips removed

50 g (2 oz) lightly salted butter

a good pinch of powdered saffron or a saffron thread
dissolved in a little water

1 tbls grenadine syrup

2 tbls acacia honey or pale runny honey

4 tbls virgin olive oil

50 g (2 oz) toasted slivered almonds

DRINK WITH

A sweet (*moelleux*) Viognier, or a Pacherenc du Vic-Bilh

SERVE WITH

Serve warm, perhaps with vanilla or almond ice cream,
or an almond biscuit.

I always like to give a lift to stoned fruit simply by adding a tangy touch of lemon juice. This recipe takes the lemon further: its chunky segments are stewed alongside segments of peach in a little butter. The lemon adds a vivacious piquancy to the gentle peach, and the heady scent of saffron and some grenadine syrup enhance their flavours. The real key to this gastronomic treat, however, is the trick of adding olive oil – of the finest quality you can afford – at the end of cooking. Slivered toasted almonds complete the presentation.

————————————

In a large sauté pan set over low heat, melt the butter and add the 24 segments of peach, the 6 segments of lemon, the saffron and the grenadine syrup. Partially cover the pan, and adjust the heat to allow the juices to murmur very gently for 20–30 minutes. During this time, do not stir or mix the ingredients, or the segments of peach may break.

When the fruit is tender yet still holding its shape, remove from the heat. Drizzle over the olive oil and sprinkle with the toasted, slivered almonds.

RHUBARB AND STRAWBERRIES
with PRALINES AND ORANGE

SERVES 4, 45 MINS

4 red-coloured stalks of rhubarb, washed and cut into 11 cm (4½ inch) sticks

250 g (9 oz) strawberries, rinsed quickly, and hulled

125 g (4½ oz) almond *pralines de Montargis*

1 orange, cut into 6–8 segments depending on size, pips removed and the skin left intact

50 g (2 oz) lightly salted butter, clarified

100 g (4 oz) caster sugar (superfine sugar)

juice of ½ lemon

DRINK WITH

A Cosmopolitan cocktail: 40 ml Vodka, 15 ml Cointreau, 30 ml cranberry juice and 15 ml fresh lime

SERVE WITH

4 scoops of good-quality vanilla ice cream; dessert biscuits such as *palmiers*, Florentines, shortbread or cookie of your choice

This is a culinary love affair of opposites: the tartness of rhubarb and the sweetness of strawberries. Just thinking about these two mingling in the warmth of melting butter and sugar, I can smell their fragrance rising from the pan. And, in my mind's eye, I can see little pearls of juice being released, red from the strawberries and pink from the rhubarb. It's a splendid partnership. Here, segments of orange and *pralines de Montargis* – almonds wrapped in caramelised sugar – come to witness the marriage and make it all the more memorable.

———————————

Put the butter in a large sauté pan, preferably with flared sides. Set it over very gentle heat and, when the butter starts to foam, add the sugar and stir the ingredients together for about 2 minutes to blend them. Add the sticks of rhubarb and the quarters of orange in a single layer without overlapping. Leave them to cook, uncovered, very gently for 20–25 minutes, turning them over carefully after 12 minutes. During the cooking of the ingredients, do not mix them, otherwise they will lose their shape and form. You should also maintain a very low heat so that the butter and sugar mixture remains light-coloured.

Add the strawberries and pieces of praline and leave them to soften – again without mixing – for about 7 minutes or until the rhubarb is tender and the strawberries are half-cooked.

To serve, transfer the ingredients to 4 warm table plates. Add the lemon juice to the pan, and stir quickly over heat to dissolve the deposits and make a sauce. Drizzle this sauce over the dessert and serve with a scoop of vanilla ice cream and a dessert biscuit.

RED PEPPERS AND BLACK TOMATOES
with CORIANDER (CILANTRO)

SERVES 4, 35 MINS PLUS 3 HRS MARINATING

2 large red peppers, cut in half lengthways, seeds and pith removed

4 black tomatoes, preferably Noir de Crimée variety, or 4 red tomatoes, cored and sliced

1 clove of garlic, peeled and very finely chopped

1 large sweet onion, very finely sliced, preferably using a mandoline

leaves from 2 sprigs of coriander (cilantro), coarsely chopped or snipped

8 tbls virgin olive oil

fleur de sel or salt of your choice

DRINK WITH

An anise-flavoured spirit like *Ricard Pastis*, or a young Mourvèdre from Bandol, served chilled

SERVE WITH

Olive bread, warm or toasted

Writing these words, I'm drooling already! It's the thought of the black tomato in league with the red pepper. What a stunning encounter. They are, after all, two big personalities from the summer vegetable garden. In this recipe, they take the leading roles, while fresh coriander and angel-hair strands of onion play secondary parts with conviction.

Even though so-called 'black' tomatoes are more of a reddish or mahogany brown than truly black, there is no doubt they have excellent flavour and good visual appeal when juxtaposed with red peppers. You may be able to find Black Prince and Black Krim as well as Noir de Crimée, which is my favourite. If you find any of these varieties difficult to source, use red tomatoes instead and include a green pepper for contrast of colour.

———————————

To make the cut halves of pepper easy to peel, first blister their skins: place them, skin-side up, on a grill-pan. Set the grill-pan beneath a hot grill for about 10 minutes. During this time, use a skewer to lift the shallow surfaces of the peppers upwards towards the heat, so as to blister the skin evenly. Wrap the blistered peppers in a cold, damp kitchen towel; after 5–10 minutes, peel off the skin and cut the flesh into strips.

Put the strips of pepper into a large salad bowl, along with the garlic, onion, coriander and tomatoes. Add the olive oil. Turn the ingredients lightly to coat them, then leave them to marinate for 3 hours.

Serve with *fleur de sel*, or other good quality salt, and toasted olive bread.

A HARLEQUIN'S GARDEN OF VEGETABLES DRESSED *with* STUFFED DATES

As colourful as the French Harlequin's costume, this dish offers a vibrant glimpse of Moroccan cuisine using some of its most characteristic elements. Although the flavourings transport us to the Maghreb, the vegetables stay closer to home.

SERVES 4, 1 HR

4 large Medjool dates, stoned

4 small beetroots (beets), preferably a mixture of a red variety and a white variety, such as Albina Veruduna

a small bunch of carrots on their stalks, weighing about 400 g (14 oz), washed

a small bunch of baby turnips of mixed varieties on their stalks, weighing about 450 g (1 lb), washed

300 ml (1¼ US cups) whole milk

60–80 g (2–3 oz) lightly salted butter

a pinch of cumin

2 dashes of virgin olive oil

1 medium to large white, sweet onion, such as a Cévennes, or a Spanish onion, finely chopped

about 4 tsp lemon marmalade

about 3 tbls (uncooked) couscous

1 tbls argan oil

1 large aubergine (eggplant), cut in half lengthways and thinly sliced into semi-circles

a firm heart of red or green cabbage, very finely chopped

6–8 tomatoes of various colours: yellow, green, orange, red or black, cored, peeled, deseeded and cut into segments

4 courgette (zucchini) flowers, cut in half lengthways

leaves from 2 sprigs of mint

leaves from 4 sprigs of fresh coriander (cilantro), coarsely chopped

DRINK WITH
Mint tea

TO SERVE AS A MAIN COURSE
Increase the quantities of vegetables and offer extra couscous as an accompaniment.

In separate saucepans of lightly salted water, simmer the beetroots, carrots and turnips in their skins to an *al dente* stage. Cool the beetroots in their cooking water, then peel them. Drain the carrots and turnips.

While the root vegetables are cooking, make the sauce: put the milk, 40 g (1½ oz) of the butter, the cumin, a dash of olive oil and the onion in a saucepan, and simmer for about 5 minutes or until the onion has softened. Blend to a sauce and keep warm in a bain-marie.

Fill the stoned dates with the lemon marmalade, then warm them through in 20 g (¾ oz) of butter in a frying pan; set aside. Cook the couscous, drain it and mix with the argan oil by hand; keep it hot, preferably in a bain-marie.

In a large frying pan, sauté the aubergine, heart of cabbage, tomatoes and courgette flowers in stages, in olive oil, for 2–3 minutes. Transfer them to a warm serving dish and add the cooked root vegetables, cutting larger specimens as you like. Season with salt and drizzle a light coating of the sauce on top. Put the dates in place.

Sprinkle couscous very lightly over the dish, so the colourful patchwork of vegetables remains visible. Garnish with the mint leaves and chopped coriander, and serve straight away.

A SUMMER MOSAIC OF
GREEN VEGETABLES

SERVES 4, 35 MINS

6 tbls virgin olive oil

leaves from ½ bunch of purple or green basil

200 g (7 oz) shelled broad beans (fava beans)

1 baby cucumber weighing about 75 g (3 oz),
deseeded and cut into small even-sized pieces

1 courgette (zucchini) weighing about 250 g (9 oz), peeled
free of thick ribs and cut into small even-sized pieces

1 green apple, cored and cut into small even-sized pieces
with the skin intact

1 lime, peeled and cut into pith-free segments

about 12 small, sweet green or yellow grapes (preferably
Chasselas grapes), cut in half

6 small pistachio macaroons, crumbled into
small pieces

fleur de sel or salt of your choice

DRINK WITH

A dry, fruity, white wine from the Loire or from Alsace,
preferably made from the Chasselas grape

This marbled mosaic of green vegetables, viewed through
glass containers, is a dream of a dish. Its translucence seems
to open up a window on today's culinary ideas about crudités.
Here, the game of texture and flavour – which includes pistachio
macaroons – is played out beneath the supreme control of a
basil-flavoured dressing. And in this visibly 'open' presentation,
each ingredient must hold its shape and its place. With this
mosaic, I invite you to a glorious summer tasting.

————————————

To make the dressing, blend together the basil leaves, olive oil
and a good pinch of salt, using an electric blender. Set it aside in
a sauce-boat.

Parboil the shelled broad beans for 3 minutes, then drain and
refresh them in cold water for 5 minutes to retain their colour.
Drain again and slip the beans free from their skins.

Put the broad beans in a large salad bowl. Add the cucumber,
courgette, apple, segments of lime and the grapes. Mix these
elements together very gently.

Transfer the assembly to 4 glass fruit dishes, ideally of a size
which allows the assembly to be piled up, proud of the dish.
Drizzle a long trail of basil-flavoured dressing over the top.
Sprinkle with the crumbled pistachio macaroons and serve.

TO SERVE AS A MAIN COURSE

Increase or double the portion size. If you do not have glass
bowls of a suitable size for individual servings, offer the 'mosaic'
from one large glass bowl. An accompaniment of nut bread goes
extremely well with this dish.

A WARM COMPOTE OF PLUMS
with HONEY AND ORANGE

**SERVES 4, 1 HR 10 MINS PLUS
10 MINS COOLING**

about 1 kg (2.2 lb) ripe plums, preferably
Reine Claude (greengages)

40 g (1½ oz) Brittany butter with sea salt crystals*

2 tbls caster sugar (superfine sugar)

2 tbls acacia honey, or pale runny honey of your
choice

1 orange cut into segments, pips removed and
skin intact

1 lemon cut into segments, pips removed and
skin intact

DRINK WITH

A sweet Chenin Blanc from the Loire: Quarts
de Chaume or Coteaux du Layon, or Montlouis
sur Loire

SERVE WITH

Quality vanilla ice cream; *palmiers* biscuits,
shortbread or the cookies of your choice

* You can concoct this special blend of butter
yourself by gradually beating a heaped teaspoon
of large-grained sea salt into 40 g (1½ oz) softened
unsalted butter.

A hot pan of softening plums with a slice of butter containing crystals of salt … it is a simple but inspirational starting point for a dessert. In France, I use the esteemed Reine Claude variety of plum – truly the queen of plums in my view. What this recipe reveals to us is that plums have a hidden penchant for travel and for the taste of citrus fruit from warmer climates. So, in this recipe, segments of orange and lemon, tenderized and sweetened by cooking, come to flavour the plums and transport them somewhere refreshingly new to our palates.

————————————

Choose a sauté pan, preferably with flared sides, large enough to eventually accommodate the plums in a single layer. Add the butter, sugar and honey. Over low heat, stir these ingredients to blend them, then add the segments of orange and lemon. Cover with a lid set askew and leave the ingredients to murmur gently and infuse for 10–15 minutes.

Add the plums, whole, to the syrup mixture, arranging them carefully in a single layer. Stew the fruit, partially covered, for 30–40 minutes or until the fruit is tender but not mushy.

Remove the pan from the heat and leave the plums to cool in the syrup for 10 minutes.

Serve the plums warm, with vanilla ice cream. Offer a sweet biscuit or cookie of some kind: lightly toasted *palmiers* are lovely with this dessert, but shortbread could also be put to good use.

TURNIPS AND BLACK TOMATOES COOKED IN BEAUJOLAIS, SERVED *with* BOILED EGGS

SERVES 4, 1 HR

2 bunches of baby mauve-tinged turnips, cut into segments or thick slices depending on their size

3 medium-sized tomatoes, preferably a so-called 'black' variety such as Noir de Crimée, Marmande, Black Prince or Black Krim, cored and cut into thick segments

1 (75 cl) bottle of Beaujolais, preferably Saint-Amour

4 eggs

about 100 g (4 oz/1 US stick/8 tbls) lightly salted butter, diced

½ bunch small onions, weighing about 100 g (4 oz), very finely sliced

2 cloves of new garlic, skinned and crushed

a pinch of *quatre épices*

a few chives, finely snipped

fleur de sel or salt of your choice

DRINK WITH

A Gamay from Beaujolais, preferably a Saint-Amour, a Morgon or a Moulin à Vent

TO SERVE AS A MAIN COURSE

Increase the portion size of the turnips and tomatoes but not necessarily the eggs. Offer an accompaniment of wholemeal or farmhouse bread. This dish might also combine nicely with a warm potato salad.

Initial thoughts about the turnip and the tomato suggest that they have little to say to each other. However, I felt obliged to find a way of making them try harder. So I found them a nice bottle of Beaujolais to share. And you will see, in this recipe, that the wine encourages the development of a very sympathetic relationship. The accompaniment of boiled eggs spreads the flavours nicely.

————————

Put the butter in a large sauté pan, preferably with flared sides. Arrange the turnips in a single layer. Add the tomatoes, onion and garlic. Partially cover the pan and let the ingredients sweat over gentle heat, without colouring, for 10–12 minutes.

Remove the lid, raise the heat slightly, add a splash of wine and continue to cook the ingredients uncovered until the wine has evaporated. Add a little more of the wine and continue in this way, taking care never to immerse the turnips, until all of the wine has been added and reduced, and the turnips are tender.

Just before the last of the wine has been added, boil the eggs until the yolks are soft or just firm, according to taste. Set these aside briefly.

Season the turnip and tomato mixture with salt, a breath of *quatre épices* and a sprinkling of chives. Arrange these ingredients on 4 warm table plates. You can either put the eggs in egg cups and place them at the side of each plate or, alternatively, you can spoon a garnish of soft egg yolk over the central ingredients and scatter the egg white, chopped finely, over the whole.

CEPS (PORCINI) *with* LEMON, THYME AND OLIVE OIL

SERVES 4, 1 HR 10 MINS

500 g (1 lb 1 oz) ceps (porcini), brushed clean, wiped with a damp cloth and cut lengthways into ½ cm (¼ inch) thick slices

1 large lemon, cut into 8 segments, pips removed, skin intact

2 tbls caster sugar (superfine sugar)

1 tbls fresh thyme, finely chopped

1 clove of new garlic, peeled and crushed

4 tbls virgin olive oil

coarse grained grey sea salt

freshly ground white pepper

fleur de sel or salt of your choice

DRINK WITH

A Médoc or Haut-Médoc from Bordeaux, 7–8 years old

SERVE WITH

A *mesclun* salad

TO SERVE AS A MAIN COURSE

Increase or double the portion size and serve with tagliatelle.

What to offer the cep, the prince of mushrooms? You will see here that a bouquet of fresh thyme and lemon *confit* makes a very nice present indeed. The cep, charmed by the elegance of the gift, and its blend of sweetness and astringency, is swept off its feet.

———————————

Choose a saucepan into which the segments of lemon will fit snugly in a single layer. Arrange them in the pan and sprinkle evenly with the sugar. Add the thyme, garlic, 2 of the 4 tablespoons of olive oil, a good pinch of grey sea salt and ground white pepper from 8 turns of the mill. Add enough water to just cover the ingredients.

Simmer the ingredients very gently for one hour, turning the segments after 30 minutes. During cooking, the water will reduce and the mixture form a syrup which will transform the segments of lemon into *confits*. If the water reduces too quickly, add a little more.

When the lemon *confits* are almost done, sauté the mushrooms in the remaining 2 tablespoons of olive oil, in a frying pan, for 3–4 minutes; season with *fleur de sel* or the salt of your choice. Arrange on a warm serving dish, and spoon over the lemon *confits*, discarding the thyme and garlic from their syrup. Decorate with a salad of *mesclun* or offer it separately. Serve immediately.

RED BEETROOT *with* LAVENDER AND CRUSHED BLACKBERRIES

SERVES 4, UP TO 1 HR 15 MINS

4 medium-sized red beetroots (beets) in their skin, uncooked

flowers from a sprig of lavender

a bowl of ripe blackberries

40 g (1½ oz/3 tbls) lightly salted butter

1 tbls soy sauce, light or regular version, according to taste

1 tbls balsamic vinegar

leaves from 4 sprigs of purple basil, or green basil if purple is unavailable, coarsely cut

½ litre (2¼ US cups) whole milk

fleur de sel or salt of your choice

DRINK WITH

A young red Pineau des Charentes served cold

This combination of beetroot and blackberry is a great delicacy – and a recipe I had to think hard about before I even dared to attempt it. It turns out that these two ingredients are made for each other. It's written in their colours, their flavours and their scents. As for the lavender, it brings a subtle flowery fragrance to the union. I warmly invite you to this marriage. It's simply beautiful.

———————————

Cook the beetroots in lightly salted simmering water, in a covered pan, for 30–60 minutes depending on size. Leave them to cool in their cooking water. When they are cool enough to handle – but still warm – slip them free of their skins and set aside.

Meanwhile, melt the butter in a sauté pan set over low heat. Add the blackberries and, after a few minutes, crush them with a fork. Continue to cook them for a further 5 minutes or until their juices flow readily. Stir in the soy sauce, the balsamic vinegar and the basil leaves, then leave the mixture to stew over the lowest possible heat without stirring for 4–5 minutes, or until it smells slightly smoky. At the same time, bring the milk just to boiling point, then whisk to emulsify it, preferably using a stick-type immersion whisk.

Turn the blackberries on to a warm serving dish and arrange the peeled beetroots on top. Spoon some of the sauce over the beetroots and drizzle the remainder over the blackberries. Add salt if desired and sprinkle with the lavender flowers.

RED CABBAGE *with* PINK GARLIC AND TARRAGON

SERVES 4, 15 MINS

1 red cabbage

2 cloves of sweet new garlic, preferably the pink-tinged variety from Lautrec, peeled and very finely sliced

leaves from 2 sprigs of fresh tarragon, finely chopped

1 green apple, cored and cut into 8 segments, skin intact

9 tbls virgin olive oil

3 tbls sherry vinegar, preferably Xérès

fleur de sel or salt of your choice

freshly ground white pepper

DRINK WITH

Rosé from Provence

The colour and structure of raw red cabbage has always intrigued me. What's more, the red ball of tightly packed leaves is an inimitable bouquet of aromas, which vary subtly from the outside leaves towards the core. For this raw cabbage salad, I had in mind a sort of firework which explodes with sparkling flavours. To achieve this effect, I use sweet pink garlic, green apple and, most importantly, a delicate touch of aniseed from fresh tarragon leaves.

———————————

Cut the cabbage into 4 or 6 segments depending on its size. Using a mandolin, or a sharp knife, cut the segments, including the white heart, into strips fine enough to resemble angel's hair.

Put the strips into a large salad bowl. Add the garlic, the tarragon, the apple, the olive oil and the vinegar. Use salad servers to lift and mix the ingredients gently and thoroughly. Season with salt and freshly ground white pepper. Serve immediately in order to preserve the crispness of both cabbage and apple. This salad is a real lip-smacker.

A TALE OF PUMPKIN AND BEETROOT

SERVES 4, UP TO 1 HR 10 MINS PLUS 40 MINS COOLING

300 g (11 oz) pumpkin, preferably butternut, cut into
4 crescent-shaped wedges

1 large, uncooked red beetroot (beet) weighing at least 700 g
(1 lb 9oz)

100 g (4 oz) lightly salted butter, preferably clarified

juice of 1 lime

leaves from 4 sprigs of mint

200 g (7 oz) Emmental cheese cut into thin slices

fleur de sel or salt of your choice

freshly ground black pepper

DRINK WITH
A Chardonnay, preferably from the Jura

SERVE WITH
Rocket salad

TO SERVE AS A MAIN COURSE
Double the portion size and serve with warm crusty bread.

This recipe brings together two sweet gems from the vegetable garden: pumpkin and beetroot. It is an encounter I did not really believe could work when I first gave it some serious thought. The practical testing in the kitchen, however, was another matter: the first mouthful confirmed a partnership of fiendish force. When the beetroot yields its fuchsia-coloured juice to the pumpkin, it is – to the eye – something splendid; to the palate, an unexpected journey.

———————————

Cook the beetroot in lightly salted simmering water, in a covered pan, for about an hour depending on size. Leave it to cool in its cooking water for about 40 minutes, then peel and cut it into large dice.

Meanwhile, select a sauté pan which will accommodate all of the ingredients and also fit beneath a grill during the last stage of cooking. Set the pan over low heat, and add the butter and the pumpkin wedges. Sweat the pumpkin gently – partially covered – for 40 minutes, or until tender and lightly coloured, turning it occasionally. Remove from the heat.

Arrange the crescents of pumpkin so that they are lying as flat as possible and distribute the diced beetroot in between, making a reasonably level layer. Add the lime juice and mint leaves, then lay the slices of Emmental on top.

Slide the pan beneath a hot grill for several minutes, or until the cheese melts. Season with salt and freshly ground black pepper. Serve immediately, preferably with a rocket salad, which will extend the flavours very nicely.

A YELLOW CARPACCIO OF ONION, POTATO, HORSERADISH AND GARLIC

SERVES 4, 30 MINS

2 large yellow onions

2–3 medium sized potatoes, skins washed and left intact

a small piece of fresh horseradish, grated

1 clove of new pink-tinged garlic, preferably from Lautrec, very finely sliced into petal shapes

8 tbls sesame oil

2–4 tbls soy sauce of your choice, either regular or light

½ tsp white sesame seeds

leaves from ½ bunch fresh tarragon, finely chopped

freshly ground black pepper

juice of ½ lemon

about 70 g (3 oz) shavings of fresh Parmesan

DRINK WITH

A dry white wine from Provence, preferably a Rolle de Provence

SERVE WITH

Toasted bread of your choice

This is my *coup de coeur* for the autumn to winter season! Just when our vegetable gardens risk becoming drab and faded, along comes pink-tinged garlic and that wonder of wonders, horseradish. Here, I use both in a happy mix of flavours, but it is the horseradish which holds the dish together and sends it to another dimension. My rule is never to go through a winter without horseradish. I love its mustardy taste, and I use it to enhance and awaken the flavours of many of our vegetable dishes, cooked and uncooked alike.

———————————

Peel and slice the onions as finely as possible, either using a mandolin or a sharp knife; discard any hard core. Set the slices aside. Simmer the potatoes in their skin for about 15 minutes or until just tender; drain. When they are cool enough to handle – but still warm – peel away their skin and slice the potatoes finely.

While the potatoes are cooking, make the dressing: mix the sesame oil with soy sauce to taste, stirring well to blend thoroughly; set this aside. To prepare the garnish, spread the sesame seeds in the bottom of a non-stick frying pan, or skillet. Set it over low to medium heat, shaking it occasionally until – after a few minutes – the seeds are evenly toasted; set these aside.

Toss the slices of onion in just enough of the dressing to coat them evenly; reserve the remaining dressing. Spread out the onions on a serving dish and arrange the sliced potatoes on top. Sprinkle with the tarragon, horseradish, freshly ground black pepper and the sesame seeds. Decorate with petals of garlic. Stir the lemon juice into the remaining dressing and drizzle it over the potatoes. Scatter with shavings of Parmesan and serve with the toasted bread of your choice.

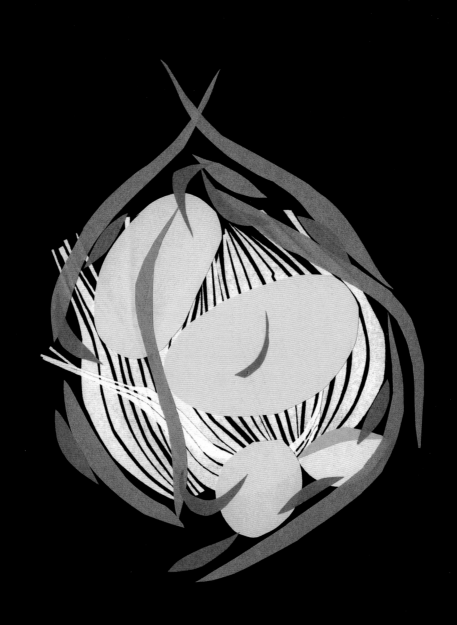

BEETROOT *with* RED ONION, BASIL AND PARMESAN

SERVES 4, UP TO 1 HR 10 MINS

2 uncooked red beetroots (beets)

1 large red onion, peeled

about 12 asparagus tips

leaves from ½ bunch of purple or green basil

a splash of balsamic vinegar

8 tbls virgin olive oil

about 1 tbls shavings of fresh Parmesan

fleur de sel or salt of your choice

freshly ground black pepper

DRINK WITH

A red Malbec from Cahors

Once again, colour leads the way in the creation of a recipe. Here, the crimson and purple shades which characterize varieties of beetroot, onion and purple Opale basil have influenced the composition of a warm salad. I draw on a unity, a resemblance in the flavours and aromas. If you cannot get hold of purple basil, then it is still worth trying with green.

This combination can stand alone with some simple seasoning or become a foundation for interesting garnishes. You can add, for example, a few asparagus tips, as here, and some shavings of Parmesan. You can also serve the dish – as indicated in the collage – with baby beetroots on their stalks. It is for you to experiment!

―――――――――――

Cook the beetroots in lightly salted simmering water, in a covered pan, for 30–60 minutes depending on size. Leave them to cool in their cooking water and when they are cool enough to handle – but still warm – peel them.

While the beetroots are cooking, prepare the other ingredients: slice the onion finely – using a mandolin if you prefer – then cut across the longer slices to make shorter strips; set these aside. Simmer the asparagus tips for a few minutes, then drain them – very carefully so as not to damage them – refresh under cold water, and drain them again.

Cut each beetroot into quarters or segments depending on size, and place them on a warm serving dish. Scatter with the onion, asparagus spears and basil. Dress with a mixture of balsamic vinegar and olive oil. Add shavings of Parmesan, and salt and freshly ground pepper to taste.

BEETROOT *with* LEEK, GREEN APPLE AND GREEN TEA

SERVES 4, UP TO 1 HR 20 MINS

4 white leeks, cut into 2.5 cm (1 inch) segments

1 large green apple, cored and cut into 8 segments with the skin intact, or a smaller one cut into quarters

½ tsp matcha green tea

4 uncooked baby red beetroots (beets) or 2 medium-sized ones

2 tbls virgin olive oil

40 g (1½ oz) lightly salted butter, preferably clarified

½ lemon, cut into very fine rounds, pips removed

soy sauce to taste

2 tbls sesame oil

1 tbls finely grated fresh horseradish

leaves from a sprig of basil

DRINK WITH
Dry white Bordeaux such as Sauvignon or Entre-Deux-Mers

TO SERVE AS A MAIN COURSE
Increase or double the portion size and serve with quinoa or couscous.

Whenever you feel like preparing an adventurous medley of ingredients, this is a go-to recipe. It's certainly out of the ordinary and, at the same time, mouth-watering and amusing. It combines vegetables, fruit and a diverse range of flavourings, including soy sauce, sesame and green tea. Increasingly, I find I cannot be without green tea in the kitchen; I adore its fragrance, as well as its taste and its whole aesthetic. Here, I use authentic matcha green tea, which is made from finely ground tencha leaves. Matcha is a brilliant addition to the store cupboard and I use it in many of my dishes.

———————————

Cook the beetroots in lightly salted simmering water, in a covered pan, for 30–60 minutes depending on size. Leave them to cool in their cooking water and when they are cool enough to handle, but still warm, peel them. Leave baby beetroots whole. Cut larger ones into quarters or segments.

While the beetroots are cooling, put the leeks in a sauté pan along with the olive oil and enough water to barely cover them. Simmer the leeks for 7–8 minutes or until cooked *al dente*. At the same time, in a small saucepan set over low heat, melt the butter and sweat the apple and the slices of lemon gently for 7 minutes, or until the apple has softened without colouring.

On a warm serving dish, make an attractive assembly of the beetroots, the pieces of leek and apple, and the rounds of lemon. Scrape up the deposits and juices in the bottom of the saucepans used to cook the apple and leeks; stir to blend and drizzle them over the assembly. Sprinkle with the matcha green tea. Season with a few drops of soy sauce to taste. Add the sesame oil in a gentle stream. Garnish with a touch of fresh horseradish and the basil leaves.

PEARS AND BLACK RADISH
with TAPENADE

SERVES 4, 35 MINS

2 ripe pears, each one cored and cut into quarters
if the pears are small or 6–8 segments if large,
the skin left intact

about 500 g (1 lb 1 oz) black radish, either several
small round ones or one large elongated one, cut
into boat-shaped segments, with the skin left intact

80 g (3 oz) lightly salted butter

juice of ½ lemon

about 50 g (2 oz) black or green olive tapenade

4 tbls virgin olive oil

shavings of fresh Parmesan

fleur de sel or salt of your choice

freshly ground black pepper

DRINK WITH
Islay Single Malt Scotch Whisky

SERVE WITH
Several handfuls of *mesclun* salad

The pear and the black radish: the contrast of their taste,
texture and colour has always intrigued me, so much that
I was inclined to believe the two elements had something
interesting to say to each other. And I wasn't wrong. First of
all, they look attractive side by side. Then, the slightly earthy,
peppery taste of the one against the sweetness of the other
will seduce the most jaded of palates.

———————————

In a saucepan set over low heat, melt half of the butter, and
add the segments of black radish with enough cold water to
half-fill the pan. Adjust the heat to maintain a light boil and
leave the radish to cook, uncovered, until all the water has
evaporated – about 15 minutes. Swirl the pan to coat the
radish in the buttery deposits and add the lemon juice.

While the radish is cooking, set a frying pan over very low
heat, and sweat the segments of pear in the remaining butter
until they colour lightly – up to 25 minutes. During this time,
turn them frequently.

Arrange the pears and radish in rows on a warm serving
dish, reserving the buttery juices from the radish. Between
the rows, add the tapenade, preferably in a 'streamer'. You
can do this either by making little blobs with a teaspoon and
joining them up, or, for a more refined presentation, you can
pipe the tapenade. Drizzle over the juices from the radish,
then add several dashes of the olive oil. Season with salt and
freshly ground black pepper, and scatter with shavings of
Parmesan. Surround with a *mesclun* salad, dressed in the
remaining olive oil.

PUMPKIN SOUP *with* BASIL AND A CAPPUCCINO TOPPING

SERVES 4, 1 HR 5 MINS

300 g (10 oz/2½ US cups) squash, such as acorn or butternut, cut into small cubes

450 ml (1 US pint) whole milk, for the soup

4 tbls virgin olive oil

leaves from a bunch of basil

fleur de sel or salt of your choice

250 ml (9 fl oz/1⅛ US cups) whole milk, for the cappuccino

DRINK WITH

A Pinot Gris from Alsace

For me, basil and squash are like sunshine and shade: they complement each other perfectly. I have always enjoyed bringing together these two ingredients, not only for their flavour but also for their appetizing colours. In this soup, the mild flavor and warmth of the squash flourishes under the scented influence of the basil. A culinary delight, smooth yet fresh-tasting. This recipe also makes a delicious dessert if you replace the cappuccino-style garnish with a cloud of whipped sweetened cream.

————————————

Put the diced squash in a casserole; cover with the milk and bring to simmering point over gentle heat. Adjust the heat to maintain a gentle simmer and cook for about 40 minutes or until the squash is tender. Remove from the heat, stir in the olive oil, basil leaves and salt, then blend in a mixer, or pass through a sieve, to obtain a smooth-textured soup of coating consistency. Add more basil leaves if required to ensure the soup has a distinctly flowery, yet refined, aroma. Set the soup aside in a warm place.

For the cappuccino, bring the rest of the milk to simmering point, then whisk it with a stick-type immersion mixer until it emulsifies and forms a rich froth; transfer to a sauce-boat.

Turn the soup into a warm tureen. Serve each portion with an island of cappuccino floating on top. Add a small basil leaf for garnish and colour.

RED TIGER BANANAS *with* MADRAS CURRY, SAGE AND ONION

SERVES 4, 40 MINS

2 firm Red Tiger bananas or mature bananas of your choice, cut into sections about 2 cm (¾ inch) thick, with the skin intact

40 g (1½ oz/3 tbls) lightly salted butter

1 large sweet onion, preferably a mauve or red variety

leaves from 2 large sprigs of sage

a good pinch of Madras curry powder

juice of ½ lemon

fleur de sel or salt of your choice

DRINK WITH
An aged Muscat de Rivesaltes Ambré

TO SERVE AS A MAIN COURSE
Double the portion size and serve with rice.

For this racy adventure with ingredients from different continents, curry unites the banana and onion, both of which welcome the warm, scented spices of the ochre-colored powder. Sage, with its elegant note of bitterness, presides over this geographically opposed meeting. This is a somewhat wayward dish in terms of textures and harmonies, but I adore it.

————————————

Peel and finely slice the onion, preferably using a mandolin. In a enamelled cast-iron casserole (or Dutch oven), melt the butter over very low heat. Add the onion and the sage leaves, and the sections of banana with their skin intact. Let the mixture sweat gently. After about 10 minutes, turn the ingredients and sweat for a further 10–15 minutes, or until the banana pieces and onion are tender – but not over-coloured – and the sage leaves are crisp.

Sprinkle the banana and onion evenly with the curry powder and *fleur de sel*. Arrange the ingredients on a warm serving dish. For the presentation, I leave the skin on the banana sections to keep them intact, but it's not for eating. Deglaze the pan with the lemon juice, stirring it into the cooking butter and blending well to make a sauce. Transfer it to a warm sauce-boat and serve the dish without delay.

BAKED APPLES *with* HIBISCUS PETALS AND CRUSHED SUGARED ALMONDS

SERVES 4, 55 MINS PLUS 40 MINS INFUSION

4 red apples

50 g (2 oz) dried hibiscus petals

40 g (1½ oz/3 tbls)) crushed sugared almonds

80 g (3 oz/⅓ cup) caster sugar (superfine sugar)

1 blood orange, cut into thin rounds, pips removed

1 clove

1 whole star anise

a pinch of freshly grated nutmeg

800 ml (1⅓ pints/ 3½ US cups) water

about 60 g (2 oz) lightly salted butter

4 thin slices of brioche or sweet bread of your choice

leaves from 2 sprigs of mint

DRINK WITH
Vintage Cider or Perry

SERVE WITH
4 scoops of quality vanilla ice cream

Here we have an exquisite dessert for Christmas. By way of a bonus, the fragrant infusion of hibiscus and traditional sweet spices, which you use to baste the apples, will also scent your home. The most generous gift comes from the hibiscus, which mingles with the more familiar flavours before transporting them to a new realm of sense experience. You can obtain dried hibiscus petals from tea specialists, health-food shops and herbalists. The beautiful red colouring of cherry hibiscus or a red variety of marsh hibiscus is the best choice for this dish.

———————————

Put the sugar in the bottom of a pan and lay the hibiscus petals on top. Add the rounds of orange, clove, star anise and nutmeg. Cover with the water and set the pan over low heat. Leave the ingredients to simmer very gently and infuse for 40 minutes, then remove from the heat. Set the infusion aside, without straining it and allowing it to cool naturally.

Core the apples, leaving their skins intact and scoring the skin lightly round the middle to prevent bursting. Spread a little of the butter over the bottom of a baking dish to accommodate the apples. Arrange the apples in the dish and distribute the rest of the butter in their cavities. Ladle over the infusion, complete with its rounds of orange and flavourings, to a depth of about 2 cm (¾ inch).

Transfer the dish to an oven preheated to 190°C (375°F, Gas Mark 5). Bake the apples, basting them regularly with the surrounding syrup, for 30–40 minutes or until tender but not mushy.

Toast 4 slices of brioche or sweet bread and distribute them to individual plates. Place a baked apple on top. If you like, place a scoop of quality vanilla ice cream at the side of each apple to make an accompaniment. Above all, make a pretty decoration: arrange mint leaves around the cavity of each apple and scatter with crushed sugared almonds. In the spirit of Christmas, garnish with the red hibiscus petals and the rounds of orange *confit*.

AVOCADO SOUFFLÉS *with* DARK CHOCOLATE

An avocado as a dessert … and, what is more, a hot soufflé in its own shell. With my great fondness for the rich creamy flesh of the avocado, I wanted to extend its range: I imagined it not only in a sweet register of flavour but also lifted out of its classical repertoire and given a more contemporary twist. This recipe reinforces its flavour with a touch of pistachio and, to crown it all, adds a sumptuous note of dark chocolate.

SERVES 4, 35 MINS

2 ripe avocados

20 small squares of dark chocolate

1 vanilla pod (bean)

a small piece of pistachio flavoured marzipan about the size of a thumb-nail

4 large egg whites

60 g (2½ oz) caster sugar (superfine sugar)

a few pinches of icing sugar (confectioner's sugar)

a pinch of salt

DRINK WITH

A fortified red wine: a grenache from Roussillon, preferably a Maury or Banyuls

Cut the avocado in half, discarding the stone. Using a teaspoon, carefully scrape out the avocado flesh without damaging the skin. Transfer the flesh to the mixing bowl of an electric blender or mixer. Place the avocado shells on a baking sheet and set aside.

Preheat the oven to 220°C (425°F, Gas Mark 7). Split the vanilla pod lengthways; scrape out its seeds and add them to the mixing bowl along with the pistachio flavoured marzipan. Blend the ingredients to a smooth purée, then transfer to a large mixing bowl.

In a separate mixing bowl – preferably made of copper – beat the egg whites together with a pinch of salt until they form soft peaks. Whisk in the caster sugar, a tablespoon at a time, and continue whisking until the mixture forms stiff but not dry peaks. Fold about a quarter of the whisked egg white into the avocado purée, then combine the purée with the remaining whites, repeatedly lifting the whites from the bottom of the bowl over the top until all is well combined.

Transfer the mixture immediately to the avocado shells. Add 5 squares of chocolate to each one, distributing them evenly and pushing them into the soufflé mixture with a skewer. Use a spatula to smooth the top into a dome shape. Bake the soufflés in the preheated oven for about 7 minutes or until fully risen. Serve immediately, lightly dusted with icing sugar.

RED APPLES AND RED CHICORY COOKED IN BUTTER AND SAGE

SERVES 4, 25 MINS

2 firm red apples, cored and cut into ½ cm
(¼ inch) segments with the skin intact

2 heads of red chicory, their leaves
separated

80 g (3 oz/6 tbls) lightly salted butter,
clarified

80 g (3 oz/6 tbls) lightly salted butter,
cut into dice

½ tsp caster sugar (superfine sugar)

freshly grated nutmeg

juice and finely grated zest of 1 lemon

DRINK WITH

A Riesling from Alsace

Once again, I am throwing into relief a hint of bitterness, this time thanks to red chicory which, to my mind, has a subtler flavour than its white counterpart. I bring to it the taste of red apple and the fragrance of sage. And the red chicory puts these elements to good use, drawing on the sugar of the first and the freshness of the second. The final word belongs to the salted butter used to cook this delicate assembly and make a silky sauce.

———————————

Choose a sauté pan or saucepan wide enough to accommodate the segments of apple in a single layer and to manoeuvre the chicory leaves easily. Set the pan over low heat and cook the segments of apple in the clarified butter for 5 minutes. Turn over the segments, then add the sugar, the chicory leaves and the sage. Continue to cook these ingredients together for a further 5 or 6 minutes or until the apple is lightly coloured.

Add the nutmeg, lemon zest and salt to taste. Let these ingredients mingle together for a few minutes, then transfer everything carefully to a warm serving dish, leaving behind buttery deposits in the bottom of the pan. Set the serving dish aside in a warm place while you make the butter sauce.

Return the cooking pan to the heat and use a wooden spoon to scrape up the sticky deposits. Add the lemon juice, then raise the heat to dissolve the deposits into the liquid, stirring all the time. Lower the heat and stir in the diced butter, bit by bit. For a smooth, homogeneous sauce, ensure that the last piece of butter has been incorporated before adding the next.

Coat the chicory and apple with the sauce to impart a pretty golden glaze. Serve straight away.

YELLOW BEETROOT BAKED IN A DOME OF COARSE SALT

SERVES 4, 1 HR 10 MINS PLUS 1 HR RESTING

4 uncooked yellow beetroots (beets) in their skins, weighing about 150 g (5 oz) each

2 kg (4.4 lb) *Gros sel gris de Guérande*, or coarse-grained sea salt of your choice

60 g (2½ oz) unsalted butter

zest and juice of 1 lemon

DRINK WITH

A dry Muscat preferably from Alsace or Roussillon

TO SERVE AS A MAIN COURSE

Increase or double the portion size and serve with goat cheese and chopped walnuts. You might also combine this dish with a warm salad of haricots verts.

This is surely the simplest recipe in the entire book. It is one where the cook stands aside and lets precision and understated elegance take their rightful place. You can use small red beetroots to replace the yellow ones used here, but if you can find them, yellow beetroots like Touchstone Gold and Burpee's Golden are the little pearls of the vegetable garden. They have a sweeter and less earthy taste than their red counterparts and they do not bleed when cut. If you cannot grow your own, they can also be tracked down at the more specialized vegetable counters or mail-order suppliers.

———————

Preheat the oven to 150°C (300°F, Gas Mark 2). Choose a baking dish to accommodate the beetroots snugly. Spread enough of the salt on the bottom of the dish to make a smooth layer. Rinse the beetroots, sit them on top of the salt bed, then cover them evenly with the remaining salt so that they disappear beneath 4 pyramids. Transfer the baking dish to the oven, carefully, so as not to disturb the salt.

After one hour, test the beetroots: a trussing needle, or a thin skewer, will sink easily into the beetroots when they have cooked sufficiently. As soon as the beetroots are done, turn off the heat and leave them to relax in the oven for a further hour with the oven door wide open.

Just before serving the beetroots, cut the butter into 4 pieces and sprinkle each piece with lemon juice and zest. To serve the dish, take it to the table with a large knife and break the block of salt in front of your fellow diners. Brush the salt from each beetroot. Cut it in half and serve it with a portion of the prepared butter. To savour the dish at its best, eat the beetroot flesh together with the skin – it is the skin which really heightens flavours here!

To serve the beetroot, a garnish of fresh herbs – a touch of chervil, for example, or some spring onion – is an optional refinement, but not honestly necessary.

A JAM OF BLOOD ORANGES, RASPBERRIES AND MINT

SERVES 4, 55 MINS PLUS COOLING

4 organically grown blood oranges

1 punnet of raspberries

35 % of the weight of the oranges in caster or fine sugar, about 350 g (12½ oz)

leaves from about 6 sprigs of fresh mint

DRINK WITH

A red, sweet, fortified dessert wine from Roussillon, preferably a Maury or Banyuls

Blood oranges and mint! I had imagined their scents and flavours crossing paths in a saucepan for quite a while. Then I thought of them coming together with raspberries. This is the delicious – and beautifully perfumed – result of my efforts, which I invite you to put in your jam pots for breakfast.

———————————

Cut the oranges in half, then cut the halves into very fine segments, retaining the skin and discarding the pips. Put the segments in a preserving pan – preferably made of copper – along with the raspberries, mint leaves and sugar.

Over low heat, stir the mixture with a wooden spoon until the sugar has dissolved. Raise the heat to bring the mixture to a vigorous boil for several minutes, then adjust the heat to maintain a simmer for 35–40 minutes. Stir from time to time to prevent sticking.

Remove the pan from the heat. When the jam is cool enough to eat, spread it on toasted brioche and eat it straight away. Alternatively, you can preserve it by ladling the mixture through a funnel into one or two sterilized jars, then sealing the jars with waxed paper and airtight lids.

CHICORY *with* ORANGE PEEL AND FRESH MINT

SERVES 4, 1 HR 10 MINS

4 heads of white chicory, leaves separated and trimmed free of core

1 head of red chicory, leaves separated and trimmed free of core

150 g (5 oz) candied orange peel

juice of 2 blood oranges

1 blood orange, peeled free of pith

leaves from 3 sprigs of mint

400 g (14 oz) firm white heart of red cabbage, finely chopped

100 g (4 oz) lightly salted butter

1 large red onion, finely chopped

125 cl (5 US cups) whole milk

2 tbls virgin olive oil

2 tbls walnut oil

balsamic vinegar

fleur de sel or salt of your choice

freshly ground black pepper

DRINK WITH

A medium-dry Vouvray

When you combine the slightly bitter edge of chicory with the sweet yet sharp taste of orange, you have a real treat. This is a dish I recall from childhood, a pleasure to make and a joy to taste. The version here transforms the element of orange into a fondue. And I've added an unctuous *mousseline* made from the heart of red cabbage. Alchemy at work!

In a partially covered saucepan set over low heat, combine 75 g (3 oz) of the butter, the orange juice and the candied orange peel, and simmer for about 25 minutes or until the peel has softened. Meanwhile, use a small sharp knife to cut segments from the orange, slicing along each side of its pithy membrane and allowing the segments to fall free.

Blend all of these ingredients to a purée using an electric blender. Pass the purée through a sieve to create a silky-textured fondue. Keep this fondue warm in a bain-marie.

To make the *mousseline,* melt the remaining butter in a sauté pan and sweat the chopped cabbage heart and onion over low heat. When the cabbage softens slightly, add the milk and simmer gently until the solids are completely soft. Using an electric blender, blend this milky mixture to a smooth purée, then add salt and olive oil, and blend it again to make a light *mousseline.* Transfer it to a second bain-marie and keep it warm.

Heat the walnut oil in a wide sauté pan. In batches, rapidly sauté the chicory leaves just long enough for them to acquire a light colouring without losing their shape. Season with salt and freshly ground black pepper and sprinkle over the mint leaves.

Arrange the chicory leaves on a warm, flat serving dish, and serve the fondue of orange and the *mousseline* of cabbage on the side in little bowls.

PINEAPPLE *with* AN OLIVE OIL, HONEY AND LIME DRESSING

SERVES 4, 15 MINS

1 large ripe pineapple, trimmed and skinned

juice of 1 lime

70 g (3¼ tbls) acacia honey or similar straw-coloured runny honey

150 ml (5 fl oz/¾ US cup) virgin olive oil

1 green apple

fleur de sel or salt of your choice

freshly ground pepper of your choice

DRINK WITH

A Jurançon, or a sweet (*moelleux*) Vouvray

A firm favorite at L'Arpège in winter, this pineapple dessert is ideal after a relatively substantial main course. To accompany what is essentially a palette of sweetness and fruit, I like to incorporate a savoury element of olive oil. I also find that the blended flavorings of greenish virgin olive oil, straw-coloured acacia honey, and lime juice give rise to a dressing the colour of celadon – the alluring willow green of Chinese porcelain. Do be generous with the dressing – the pineapple will lap it up. During summer months, the dressing is equally delicious with large strawberries, cut in half.

Before you start, make sure that the honey, lime juice and olive oil are at room temperature. Then, in a bowl, mix together the honey and lime juice until they are completely emulsified. Gradually whisk in the olive oil, a few drops at a time, just as you would if making a mayonnaise. Whisk until you have a smooth, homogeneous sauce, dense enough to coat a spoon; set aside at room temperature.

Stand the pineapple on its base. With a large sharp knife, slice through it vertically three times, cutting the flesh into three long sections and leaving behind the core; discard the core. Slice the sections into near-pyramid shapes and set aside.

Just before serving, halve and core the apple and slice it, preferably with a mandolin, into thin, almost transparent slices with the skin intact. Give the dressing a final whisk and spoon a round of it on to each serving plate. Arrange the pineapple pieces on top and spoon over more of the dressing. Decorate with the slivers of apple. Add the lightest touch of *fleur de sel* and freshly ground pepper, and serve straight away.

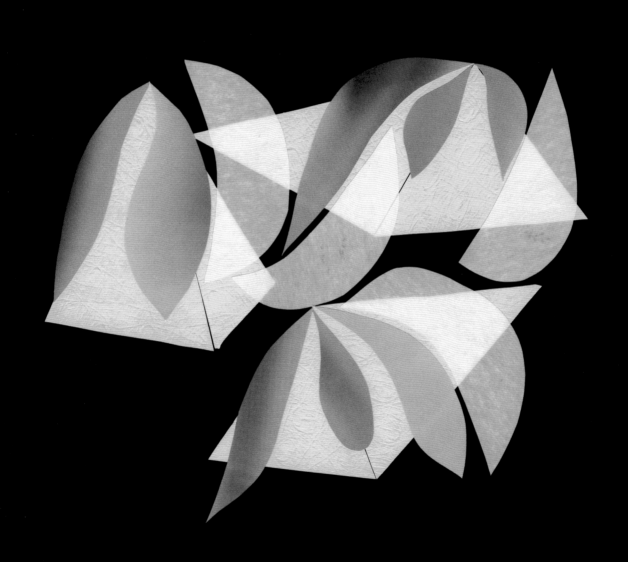